LIBRARY AUTOMATION AND DIGITIZATION

LIBRARY AUTOMATION AND DIGITIZATION

Dr. P. Balasubramanian
M.A., M.B.A., M.C.A., M.L.I.Sc., M.Phil., PGDPR, Ph.D.
University Librarian, Manonmaniam Sundaranar University
Tirunelveli 627012, Tamil Nadu, India

Dr. Sherin Yohannan
MLISc, UGC-NET, JRF, Ph.D
Librarian-UGC, Maharaja's College
Ernakulam (Kerala)

Ess Ess Publications
New Delhi

LIBRARY AUTOMATION AND DIGITIZATION

ISBN : 978-93-87698-75-8

Price : Rs. 875/-

First Published 2021

Published by:
Ess Ess Publications
4831/24, Ansari Road,
Darya Ganj,
New Delhi-110 002.
INDIA
Phones: 23260807, 41563444
Fax: 41563334
E-mail: info@essessreference.com
www.essessreference.com

Cover Design by *Patch Creative Unit*

Printed and bound in India

Dedicated to
all the
LIBRARY AND INFORMATION SCIENCE STUDENTS AND PROFESSIONALS

Contents

Preface

Library Automation and Digitization though not a recent concept, it is evergreen as all the libraries in the developing countries are in the process of automating in-house operations irrespective of their type and size. Library automation is considered as advantageous in standardizing bibliographic records and relieving libraries from the tedious as well as repetitive processes. Until recently the automation was optional activity for libraries and limited to few larger libraries with fewer operations like cataloguing, circulation of books etc. The concept has been gaining prominence in recent times and drawing the attention of most of the practicing librarians and LIS schools in developing countries including India. Moreover, it is made mandatory by the government departments, quality assessment as well as accrediting agencies, which have been encouraging foundations/consortia to design and develop LIS software for the benefit of their member libraries. For example UGC INFLIBNET has developed SOUL software and supplying to university/college libraries at nominal costs while providing training facilities for automating their in-house operations. Many commercial as well as open source LIS software have already entered the field with varied processes, facilities and customizable options, example: Libsys, Libris, Newgenlib, Koha, VTLS, e-grandhalaya, SOUL etc.

Dr.P. Balasubramanian
Dr. Sherin Yohannan

Acknowledgements

Inspiration and intuition we get from our Honourable Vice-Chancellor Prof. Dr. K. Pitchumani to write this book in a successful way is immense. We express our heartfelt gratitude to him.

We express our thanks to all those who have been very helpful in the successful completion of this book. Our sincere thanks to Dr.S. Santhosh Baboo, Registrar, Manonmaniam Sundarnar University for his support and guidance at every stage of this work. We appreciate Dr. A. Tirumagal, Librarian and Dr. K. Kannan, Assistant Librarian, Department of Library and Information Science, Manonmaniam Sundaranar University for their cooperation.

We take this opportunity to solemnly submit our gratitude to all the Staffs of Manonmaniam Sundaranar University Library, Maharaja's College Library, Teaching and Non-teaching Staffs of Manonmaniam Sundaranar University, Tirunelveli and Maharaja's College, Ernakulam for giving us constant encouragement for writing this book.

We may fail in our duty if we do not thank the services of the Publisher for their efforts in bringing out this book in a record time.

We express our sincere obligations to our Family Members who have supported us emotionally for the successful completion of this work. Our pranams to all Elders and Teachers.

Dr. P. Balasubramanian
Dr. Sherin Yohannan

About the Book

Library Automation and Digitization: Concepts, Tools and Approaches brings to the forefront the increasing recognition of the value of knowledge and information to individuals, organizations, and communities, providing an analysis of the concepts of Library Automation and Digitization that prevails among the Library and Information Science (LIS) community.

Thus, the book explores knowledge management from the perspective of LIS professionals. Furthermore, unlike most books on the topic, which address it almost exclusively in the context of a firm or an organisation to help gain a competitive advantage, this book looks at Library Automation and Digitization in the context of not for profit organisations such as libraries.

About The Authors

Dr. P. Balasubramanian is presently working as an University Librarian and Research Guide in Manonmaniam Sundaranar University, Tirunelveli (Tamil Nadu). He has completed his M.C.A.,M.B.A., M.A, (Eng.) M.A., (His.) MLISc, M.Phil, PGDPR and Ph.D. He is a life member of various Professional Associations. His books on Library and Information Science is very popular among the research scholars and library professionals. He has contributed 66 books Library and Information Science and General Books, around 150 papers in Seminars, conferences and refereed journals. He has organized many seminars and workshops in various emerging topics of Library and Information Science. He has produced 9 M.Phil and 28 Ph.D scholars, presently guiding 8 Ph.D., scholars. He has been teaching Library and Information Science for 21 years.

Dr. P. Balasubramanian is the University Librarian of Manonmaniam Sundaranar Univesity, Tirunelveli-627 012, Tamil Nadu. He holds M.A., MLISc, MPhil, MCA, MBA, PGDPR and Ph.D. He is a life member of various professional bodies. His books on Library and Information Science are very popular among the research scholars and library professionals. He has published 49 books on Library and Information Science and on General topics. He has presented 117 papers in seminars , conventions, conferences and referred journals. He has organized many National and International Seminars and workshops on various emerging topics of Library and Information Science. He is also guiding M.Phil and Ph.D research scholars in Library and Information Science. He has produced 9 M.Phil and 26 Ph.D scholars . At present he is guiding 6 Ph.D scholars. He has been teaching Library and Information Science for 19 years.

Part I : Library Automation and Digitization

1
Library Automation Packages

STRUCTURE

1.0. OBJECTIVES

- To provide access to information at a faster rate.
- To share the resources through library networking.
- To implement new IT processes to provide high quality information.

1.1. INTRODUCTION

Library Automation refers to the use of computers to serve the needs of library users. The operations of a library get a quantum jump with the introductions of computers. The computers help to provide fast and reliable access to the resources available in the library as well as elsewhere. The application of computers in the library operations avoids repetitive jobs and saves lot of labour, time, speeds up operations, increases use of library resources. Computers are not only used as a tool for processing the data, but also for data storage and accessing. Planning for an automated system, no matter how big or small, should be part of an overall long-range plan for the library. Automation should always be used as a means to achieve overall better patron service. Careful planning for technology will assure that your automation project is "sustainable", i.e. enhances the organisation's ability to meet its service mission without disrupting the organisational stability of the institution.

1.2. HISTORY AND DEVELOPMENT OF LIBRARY AUTOMATION

A process of great change has been taking place today in libraries due the impact of information technology and application of computers in library work. We hear a lot about library automation in libraries and library automation is nothing but application of machines viz. computers to the routine library housekeeping operations such as acquisition, serial control cataloguing and circulation.

The effects of ICT on libraries and information centers are characterised by:

- Mechanisation – doing what we are already doing more efficiently.
- Innovation – experimenting with new capabilities, that the ICT makes possible.
- Transformation – fundamentally altering the nature of the library operations and services through the capabilities extended by ICT.

It could be said that library automation began in 1930's when punched card equipment was implemented for use in library circulation and acquisition. The computer technology first arrived in libraries in the late 1960s in the form of locally developed software or commercial packages intended to automate library processes. The whole phase of library automation development i.e., 1960 to date may be grouped into four distinct eras:

First Era : This era is characterised by computerisation of library operations by utilizing either commercial automation package or software developed in house. The development of shared copy–cataloguing system is another significant achievement of this phase that utilised computer and communication technologies for collaboration and cooperation within the library community.

Second Era : This period of library automation is characterised by the rise of public access i.e., the arrival of OPAC as a replacement for the traditional card catalogue. This period also saw major developments in online access to abstracting and indexing databases, union catalogues, resource sharing networks and library consortia.

Third Era : This era is characterised by the full text access to electronic documents over high-speed communication channels. The advent of Internet as global publishing platform and largest repository of information bearing objects revolutionised the ways and means of delivering library services.

Fourth Era : It is known as 'networked information revolution' era. This era supports a vast variety of digital contents and services that are accessible through the network at any time, from any place, can be used and reused, navigated, integrated and tailored to the needs and objectives of each user. Digital libraries, multimedia databases and virtual libraries are major achievements in the present era.

The above discussion clearly indicates that in the first era of automation, libraries were largely stand-alone; in the second era, they became reliant on campus networking strategies; in the third era, the libraries were critically dependent on both LAN and WAN for patron access to library services. In the fourth era, libraries are not only offering their own network-based services but also becoming increasingly involved in the management and organisation of external activities on the network. As a direct result of these developments, LMSs also changed considerably through four different generations.

1.3. NEED FOR LIBRARY AUTOMATION

From the above definitions, we can say that the need of library automation has several reasons. Need of computers is present in all areas depending upon its usage. They range from acquisition control, serial control, and cataloguing and circulation control. They are also used for library manager's evaluation of reports, statistics, etc. For the good administration of the library computers are used in all levels of work. Above all, the unique characteristics of computer made it the right choice for the library world. Computers right from the beginning are considered to aid man, in doing various operations.

1.3.1. Advantages of Library Automation

Many activities of a library are routine in nature; a

few are repetitive. Automation of these activities helps in managing the library's resources in a better way at the same time saving time, money and manpower. For example, once the bibliographic details like author, title, edition, publisher, price, ISBN number, etc are entered at the time of ordering, the same data can be used for accessioning, cataloguing (OPAC), and circulation. Other important factors associated with automation are speed, and accuracy. One can imagine the time saved in literature researches and in preparing bibliographies. Automation also offers freedom from doing repetitive and routine works as well as enables providing efficient services properly and more efficiently cutting down time and improving productivity Automation also facilitates generation of a number of reports for better decision making in the effective management of the library. Availability of various statistical and other usage reports and performance reports will ensure better appreciation from library users. For example, vendor performance analysis is possible. Subject-wise or project department-wise budget can be monitored. Circulation data can provide information on titles that are in great demand so that more copies can be procured if needed. Many current awareness services like current additions, contents of books and journals, etc can also be provided to users.

1.3.2. Implementing Library Automation

Library automation, which started in late 70's in few special libraries, has now reached the university libraries. It is yet to take off in college libraries in India. Library automation refers to the use of computers in the routine and important services of a library. Automation of a library has mainly two components, viz. computerization and networking. Computerization will help a library to modernize its in-house operations while networking will allow it to access other libraries for the exchange of information.

1.4. BASIC REQUIREMENTS FOR LIBRARY AUTOMATION PACKAGES

A library automation package or LMS should fulfill the expectations of library users, staff and authority in terms of delivery, installation, implementation, maintenance, data conversion, services, utilities, training and other essential requirements for an integrated library management system. Libraries would like to develop or purchase a LMS that provides the most forward-looking, flexible, extensible and cost efficient solution. The basic requirements for any modern library automation package to satisfy such expectations may be studied under two broad categories - general system requirements and functional requirements.

1.4.1. General System Requirements

These are applicable to all modules of any modern LMS and should include but not limited to the following features:

- The LMS must be fully integrated, using a single, common catalogue database for all operations and a common operator interface across all modules.
- The LMS should have capability of supporting multiple branches or independent libraries, with one central computer configuration sharing a common database.
- The LMS must allow unlimited number of records, users and organization specific parameters (e.g. loan period rules, fine calculation criteria, hold parameters etc.).
- The package should include following fully developed and operational facilities at multiple customer sites:
  - Bibliographic and inventory control
  - Reservation and materials booking
  - Authority control

- — Circulation control
- — Public access catalogue
- — Customized generation of reports and usage statistics
- — Web catalogue interface
- — One step administrative parameters setting
- — Information gateway (telnet, www,z39.50, proxy server, external access, customized web portal)
- — Acquisition management
- — Serials control
- — Z39.50 server (minimum version 3 and path profile level complaint)
- — Electronic data interchange (EDI)
- — Z39.50 OPAC and staff client
- — Z39.50 copy cataloguing client
- — Marc 21 bibliographic and authority
- — Inter library loan record import/export utility
- — Bills and fines
- — Outreach services
- — Multimedia files
- — Digital media archive
- — Interoperability and system crosswalk
- — Fund accounting

1.4.2. Functional Requirements

These are the minimum essential features to be supported by each functional units or modules of any modern LMS:

Authority Control : The LMS must be capable of incorporating the following features:

- Support for MARC authority format for personal, corporate and topical name headings in a name authority file; title, uniform title and series entries in a title authority file, and subject headings in a subject authority file.

- Provision for generation of SEE, SEE ALSO references and Narrow Term- Broad Term-Related Term relationships network from authority records and link these references to matching access points in OPAC.
- Must allow any bibliographic field to be authority controlled, and include facilities to search, retrieve, and display print and global editing of authority records by authorised operators; and
- Must include provision for multiple thesauri with the ability to produce a list of all citations with authority file violations.

Bibliographic Control : The master bibliographic record of the LMS should extend support for:

- MARC 21 bibliographic and authority record formats.
- MARC record loader that can accept records input from various sources and from various media like tape, diskette or over network.
- Global editing utility that can find and replace data within specified fields.
- Data format validation during input of bibliographic information.
- MARC 21 format for holding and display of holding on the basis of ANSI Z39.44 serials holdings display format.
- Import and export of bibliographic data through Z39.50 compliant catalogue.
- Interoperability and crosswalk through incorporation of XML, RDF and metadata schemas (e.g. Dublin Core Metadata).

Online Public Access Catalogue (OPAC)

- OPAC must be fully integrated with other modules

and accessible through web-based client

- OPAC should provide browse indexes for author, title, and series and browse index combining all four indexes.
- It should allow combined, specific and field level searching for all formats along with phrase searching, nested searching and truncated searching.
- It must enable searching by using Boolean operators (OR, XOR, NOT, AND), positional operators (SAME, WITH, NEAR, ADJ) and relational operators ('greater than', 'less than', 'equal to', etc.) within and across all fields.
- It should provide facility to see processing status (fully catalogued, in process, lost, withdrawn etc.) and circulation status (in transit, reserve, recalled, on-hold etc.).
- OPAC should support full, brief, standard and customised display of records including relevancy ranking of search results.
- OPAC should also support bulletin board, information desk and gateway services (to access external databases) along with patron self-service options (e.g. holds, renewals etc.).
- OPAC must track user's preferences and interests, organised into a list of favorites. These favourites shall be included in a user's personal online account.

Circulation Control : The circulation control activities of any modern LMS must be supported with:

- Entry of borrower and item identification by scanner, RFID reader or keyboard entry at any workstation.
- A template for user's registration and automatic display of patron data.
- Automatic blocks for membership expiration, exceeding loan threshold, renewal threshold and fine

threshold, placement of hold on any title or item in the database.

- Automatic calculation of loan period in hours, days, weeks or months.
- Generation of notices/reminders to users of overdue items and printing of gate pass for issued items. Automatic calculation of fines and other charges, recording of payment and generation of receipts.
- Generation of variety of pre-defined and user defined reports and usage statistics; and
- Fully operational Interlibrary loan module, patron initiated transaction and mechanised inventory control (barcode, RFID, smart card etc.).

Acquisition Control : A fully integrated acquisition module of any modern LMS should support:

- All traditional acquisition activities like pre-order searching, ordering, claiming, cancellation of order, receipt processing, payment, routing, fund accounting, vendor accounting, currency control, statistics and report compilation etc. Linkage between acquisitions, cataloguing and circulation module must be seamless.
- Accommodation of a variety of materials, including but not limited to monograph, series, serials, newspapers, cumulative indexes, loose leaf materials, supplements, reports and statutes, musical scores, electronic resources etc.
- Processing of a variety of materials, including but not limited to print, Introduction microfilm, microfiche, film, videotape, audiocassette, magnetic tape, CDROM, DVD-ROM etc.
- Recording, storing and displaying of bibliographic information, acquisition type (order, gift, approval etc.), status (ordered, received etc.) invoice and accounting information, vendor information, requestor information, subject code etc.

- Budget-based fund accounting with categorised fund allocation.
- Generation of vendor performance statistics and other reports.
- Accommodation of different order types such as firm order, prepayment, exchange, membership, gift, on approval, blanket order, standing order, subscription, continuation, deposit account etc.
- Production of various customised and predefined reports as MIS activities.

Serials Control

- The module should have all the basic capabilities like ordering, check-in, claiming, routing, vouchering, fund accounting, union listing, bindery preparation and report generation.
- It should provide the ability to search for serials records by title, ISSN, publisher, vendor, purchase order, uniform title, editor, conference title, keywords etc.
- Serials control module should have provision for article indexing, online acquisition, e-journal directory service and recording of holding information.
- It should support both predictive and non-predictive modes of check-in and auto-generation of claims for non-receipted issues.
- The module should support routing of journal issues and generation of various lists and reports.

Outreach Services : An outreach services module should be available to automate the process required to:

- deliver materials to patrons who cannot physically enter the library.
- create patron interest profiles and reading histories.
- initiate easy selection, delivery and return of items;

and

- deliver local history collection and community information services.

Digital Media Archive System (DMA) : The aim of DMA subsystem is to support search, retrieval and viewing of multiple media formats from client machines by using a web browser. It should be able to:

- browse and search (full text and metadata based) contents of text and images in ASCII, HTML, SGML, PDF, TIFF, JPEG, GIF, BMP, PCX, DCX etc. formats, audio and video clips and streaming audio and video.
- Link itself with library OPAC through electronic access field (MARC/ UNIMARC 856 field).
- receive and register published documents from an electronic document management system.
- help a user to import one or more files from the user's system and associate them with a metadata schema within the archive.
- support metadata harvesting by using Open Archive Initiative (OAI)/ Protocol for Metadata Harvesting (PMH).
- extend support for various Document Object Identifier (DOI) schemes; and
- accommodate remote document submission system.

Need and Purpose : Even though this question seems to be very fundamental it is essential to emphasize this aspect, as the library automation is yet to take off in majority of the Indian libraries. Secondly, while justifying need for library automation more than cost-effectiveness the benefits derived by the library users become the major consideration. To appreciate the advantages it becomes necessary to highlight the different levels of library automation.

Following are considered as important factors for Library Automation

- Information explosion
- Increase in the collection of libraries
- Inability of users to explore the unlimited literature and information of their interest
- Advances in the computer and communication technology
- Wastage of user / staff time in locating the information
- Provide wide access to resources within the libraries and elsewhere
- Better access
- Quality in service
- Cooperative efforts (Resource Sharing)

Out of all libraries an academic library has a difficult task of defining its mission and operating objectives. The automation programme will have to manage a wide range of literature associated with numerous departments and educational programmes of the academic institution. Furthermore, in an academic library the collections will be diverse unlike a special research library where the collection is relatively homogeneous. The user group will also range widely, including faculty, staff, students, scholars, administrators and the general public. The position of an academic library funded largely by the government further complicates the process of identifying and prioritizing objectives. As difficult as the task might at first appear, it is nevertheless essential to the process of establishing automated systems of any type. In addition the overall health of one's library operation will benefit from a modicum of intellectual rigor in this area.

1.4.3. Areas of Library Automation

As a first step in a planning process, it is desirable to formulate a model for computerisation listing all itemized and prioritized information systems being maintained on a manual basis by the library. For this exercise it is necessary to break down these procedures into their constituent parts. When further subdividing these activities, each item is to be considered of its functional elements. The systems and subsystems listed below are only indicative and may vary with differing library system environments.

These are:

- Acquisitions
- Selection
- Ordering
- Claiming/cancellation
- Receiving/invoice processing
- Extended procurements
- Gift tracking
- Fund Control
- Maintains information about all library related funds
- Ability to group funds (nesting)
- Track fund allocations and adjustments
- Fund encumbrance
- Fund expenditure
- Cash Balance
- Free Balance
- Automatic updating of fiscal information through recording of specific transactions
- Track year-to-date expenditures
- Create Purchase Orders
- Technical Services
- Books
- Serials
- Special Collections
- Cataloguing

- Books
- Serials
- Special Collections
- Circulation
- Charge/Renewal
- Discharge
- Loan Periods
- Processing schedules
- Holds
- Messages
- Blocks
- Notices
- Transaction Recording Devices for off-line processing
- Member control
- Inventory Control
- Serials Control
- Receipt (check-in)
- Claiming
- Bindery control
- Replacements
- Monographic serials
- Invoice processing
- Reference Services
- Desk services
- User tools
- Bibliographic utilization
- Reprography
- Inter-library communications
- General Administration
- Grants Administration
- Library Publications

- Bindery
- Periodical Citation Searching
- OPAC
- Bibliographic Database

1.4.4. Planning of Library Automation

Planning for library automation has been defined as planning for "integrated systems" that computerize an array of traditional library functions using a common database. While this is still generally true, rapid technological change is forcing a reexamination of what it means to "automate the library." As physical, spatial and temporal barriers to acquiring information are crumbling, libraries must plan for a broader and more comprehensive approach to providing automated services.

1.5. FEATURES OF LIBRARY AUTOMATION SOFTWARE AVAILABLE IN INDIA

The automation of library activities in India started in full swing with the introduction of CDS/ISIS. CDS/ ISIS is a menu-driven generalised information storage and retrieval system designed by a team of experts under UNESCO/ PGI programme. It is specifically meant for the structured non-numerical Introduction databases. In India, erstwhile NISSAT (ceased existence since 2004) with the help of other professional bodies organised a number of training courses on application of CDS/ISIS (DOS and Windows version) in information organisation activities. As a result, a large pool of trained manpower developed all over the country. Some organizations from the experience of use of CDS/ ISIS, MINISIS etc. developed their own LMSs e.g. DESIDOC developed DLMS (Defence Library Management System), INSDOC (now NISCAIR) came with CATMAN (Catalogue Management) and SANJAY was developed by DESIDOC under NISSAT project by augmenting CDS/ISIS (Version 2.3) for library management activities. The LMSs presently available in

India may be ranked in 2nd, 3rd and in between 3rd and 4th generations on the basis of their features. As far as the origin and application domain is concerned, the LMSs available in India may be grouped into three fundamental groups – LMSs of foreign origin, LMSs developed over LMSs or textual database management systems of foreign origin and LMSs of Indian origin. This grouping may again be sharpened by dividing the packages on the basis of size of library systems i.e. large library system, medium range library system and small range library system.

1.5.1. Development of Library Automation Software in India

While the software industry is a well-organized sector, library software is largely confined to some premier institutions and their libraries. It is only recently that private sector entered this field. Even then, the aggressive marketing efforts as in the case of computer software are not there. Many of the library automation efforts using in-house expertise were around the existing PCs and software packages including dBase, and FoxPro. In some cases, high level programming languages like COBOL, BASIC, C, C++ and Pascal were used. Initially, only simple and important functions such as acquisitions, circulation and cataloguing only were automated; integrated packages were thought at a later date. These efforts generally led to the development of a total integrated system (as in ISAC and DESIDOC), or were used to convince the authorities to purchase a library automation software from the market. In some cases, the vendor of the library automation software helped to convert the automated data into a compatible form for use with the new software. Firms like LibSys undertook creation of bibliographic records of the library holdings. Both the MARC and CCF formats are used now to develop bibliographic databases.

After the introduction of CDS/ISIS software package of UNESCO in Indian libraries in the mid1980s, NISSAT organized a number of training programmes on application of CDS/ISIS to library activities in 1990s. These courses, besides training the professionals in using the software, have made them aware of the benefits of library automation and also introduced computer culture among the LIS professionals. This also gave impetus to many institutions for developing their own library software suitable for their libraries with special emphasis on the routines and services important to the institution. Thus began the indigenous efforts towards developing integrated library software packages in the country.

Some of the special libraries such as those at Bharat Heavy Electricals Ltd (R&D), Steel Authority of India Ltd (SAIL), International Crops Research Institute for the Semi-Arid Tropics (ICRISAT), INSDOC, NIC, DESIDOC, and IIT, Kanpur have successfully developed software for library automation. Specific mention is to be made of DESIDOC, which has developed three software packages. The first was named the Defence Library Management System (DELMS) and was developed in COBOL under multi-user UNIX environment. This software was provided to the DELNET, and later to INFLIBNET under the name ILMS, Integrated Library Management System. While DELNET switched over to Libris and DELSIS subsequently, INFLIBNET has developed a new soft package SOUL, Software for University Libraries. DESIDOC also developed a software package for NISSAT called Sanjay, integrated library management software using UNESCO's CDS/ISIS in Pascal language. Later DESIDOC developed Suchika, an integrated software package in C++ language. The first version was developed in DOS and UNIX platforms to suit small and large libraries. Later, Suchika version 2 was also developed on Windows NT platform. The Computer Maintenance Corporation Ltd (CMC), a public sector company specialized in computers, developed an integrated software package called Maitrayee suitable in library network environment. The software was developed with NISSAT support for CALIBNET. INSDOC initially developed CATMAN to support cataloguing in the National Science Library. Recently, it developed Granthalaya, an integrated library automation software package.

These institutional efforts inspired the software developing firms in private sector with the result that now many commercial software packages have been developed and marketed. Appendix 1 lists some software packages currently available in the country; the list is only indicative and not exhaustive.

1.5.2. Some Library Software Packages Available In India

The library application software, integrating all the activities and routines of the library is essential software for the libraries. There are many integrated library management packages available in the market suiting to the needs as well as budgets. They range from Rs. 10,000 to 6, 50,000. Many are also available in multi-user network versions. Many authors have attempted comparative study, evaluation and selection criteria for Indian software packages (see for example, Malwad, 1995; Patel and Bhargava, 1995; and Saxena and Srivastava, 1998). Chowdhury and Chowdhury (1994) reported 19 software packages used for the automation of library activities in 1994. A brief account of some of the well-known software packages is presented in the following paragraphs.

Alice for Windows : Soft Link's Alice (Windows version) is a fully integrated library management solution. The DOS version is known by OASIS. Alice for Windows is the complete library automation toolkit, which incorporates the latest information technology, and functional depth, provides a complete range of library functions using discrete modules, and allows select modules that suit the individual library need. It has wide usage and currently being used by more than 8,700 libraries all over the world. In this dynamic world of information, it follows constant features upgrade enabling to meet all kind of requirements of all range of libraries. Modules are grouped into Standard modules, Advance modules and Special modules.

Standard Modules are required for a library to function from day to day. These are: Management, Reports and Utilities, Circulation and Inquiry (OPAC). Advance Modules extend the usability of the automated library. These are: Acquisitions, Periodicals, Communications, Guidelines, Journal Indexing and Remote Inquiry. Special Modules are available for those libraries which have a specialized need. These are: Advanced Bookings, Book Review, Cooperative Cataloguing, Multimedia, Multi Lingual, Patron Self Checking, Rapid Retrospective, Remote Cataloguing, Resource Rental, Technical Manual, User Access Menu, User Definable MARC, Web Inquiry, Books Hire, CD-ROM Loader, Fines, Library Service, Interlibrary Loans, Professional Inquiry, Records Management, Report Generator, Self-Circulation, Union Catalogue, User Definable Databases, Book Wizard Cont, Mobile Circulation.

Features

- It has four versions: Academic Library. Special Library, Public Library, and School Library versions.
- It runs on Standalone PCs irrespective of the platform including Windows, Novell, Linux, with an Apple Mac version.
- It supports 239.50 clients/server architecture, GUI, intranet inquiry and system functions; Internet inquiry functions for operating systems including UNIX.
- Export and import of data in MARC formats and data conversion from CDS/ISIS, dBase, FoxBase, and from any other standard library software.
- It is multilingual and can work with such languages

as English, Russian, Japanese, Chinese, Arabic, Spanish, French, Malaysian, Vietnamese, Thai, Hindi and other Indian languages.

- The software is being continuously upgraded; one or two upgrades are being released every year.

CDS/ISIS

CDS/ISIS stands for Computerized Documentation Services/lntegrated Set of lnformation Systems. CDS/ISIS is an advanced non-numerical information storage and retrieval software developed by Unesco since 1985 to satisfy the need expressed by many institutions, especially in developing countries, to be able to streamline their information processing activities by using modern (and relatively inexpensive) technologies. The software was originally based on the Mainframe version of CDS/ISIS started in the late '60s, thus taking advantage of several years of experience acquired in database management software development.

CDS/ISIS is a menu-driven generalized information Storage and Retrieval system designed specifically for the computerized management of structured non-numerical databases. One of the major advantages offered by the generalized design of the system is that CDSI/ISIS is able to manipulate an unlimited number of databases each of which may consist of completely different data elements. Although some features of CDS/ISIS require some knowledge of and experience with computerized information systems, once an application has been designed the system may be used by persons having had little or no prior computer experience. For advanced users having access to computer professionals, CDS/ISIS offers an integrated programming facility allowing the development of specialized applications and/or the functional extension of the software as originally provided.

It has the largest installed base of about 1390 installations (Kittur, 1998, p. 4) and is a PC version available on a number of platforms like Windows 95, Windows NT, DOS, Claris etc. It has a number of fields, records, alternate scripts, multimedia capability, and Web interface. Many specialized application products have been developed around CDS/ISIS (Sanjay and Trishna library software packages, for example). Besides in libraries, the package can be equally used to create databases. An ideal software package for small and medium-size libraries, it was distributed free of charge initially; now it is priced at Rs 1500/- onwards. The package performs a variety of operations related to information storage and retrieval with powerful search capabilities and flexible database management. It allows interlinking records from more than one database, use of more than one data sheet, and conforms to 180-2709. The major functions provided by CDS/ISIS allow you to:

- Define databases containing the required data elements
- Enter new records into a given database
- Modify, correct or delete existing records
- Automatically build and maintain fast access files for each database in order to maximize retrieval speed
- Retrieve records by their contents, through a sophisticated search language
- Display the records or portions thereof according to your requirements
- Sort the records in any sequence desired
- Print partial or full catalogues and/or indexes
- Develop specialized applications using the CDS/ISIS integrated programming facility.

DELMARC and DELPLUS

DELPLUS (formerly DELSIS), an integrated modular package, was developed on Basis plus by DELNET to support complex cataloguing and union catalogue functions under network environment. The software provides interface to CDS/ISIS and supports creation of bibliographic records in 13 Indian languages (using GIST card). It facilitates duplicate checking, online help and interlibrary loan. Currently it supports all the DELNET databases catering to all the network users. The software is ISO2709 compatible. While DELMARC is designed for bigger libraries that have collections of more than one lakh, DELPLUS is designed for all types of small libraries with a collection of up to one lakh.

Special Features

- Software is compatible with bar code technology.
- It is designed and developed exclusively to work in all kinds of libraries including public libraries, academic libraries and special libraries.
- Multi-user facility allows different branch libraries/ sections/nodes of a library to function together.
- Free up gradation available.
- Follows internationally recommended standards and formats such as US-MARC, MARC21, UNIMARC, and UK-MARC.
- Provision for backlog entry, backup and restore facility and bar coded stock verification facility.
- Provides lists of country and language codes and also online help.
- DELPLUS Ver 1.0.0
- DELPLUS is menu driven with Graphical User Interface (GUI). It is a user-friendly tool.
- It has an effective administration and security system and provides for password both for system Administrator as well as the User.
- Follows internationally recommended formats such as MARC-21, US MARC and CCF.

- Best for smaller libraries which have collections up to one lakh holdings.
- Reservation facility for materials.
- Online monitoring of the status of material.
- Interactive facility for maintaining library inventory/ database.
- Generation of reminders and intimations to the Members.
- Generation of reminders to vendor, supplier, binder, etc.
- Advanced backup and recovery system.
- Online listing of country and language information with related codes.
- Online Help system for all modules.

This software comprises Acquisition, Cataloguing, Circulation, OPAC Search, Article Indexing, Authority Control Systems, and System Administration modules.

Grandhalaya

Grandhalaya is an integrated software package for library Information systems designed specifically to meet all needs of general as well as special libraries by Ananth Technologies Pvt Ltd of Hyderabad. It handles large, text-intensive and unlimited number of records and provides fast access on free text searches and eases the tasks of acquisition, cataloguing, circulation and information management. It is a friendly package to both the librarians and users. It has been developed using the most advanced technologies and tools like Visual Basic HTML, DHTML, ASP and JavaScript and VBScript to make the application platform independent and portable to web browsers. It is also compatible with Oracle, MS-SQL Server, MS-Access etc. and is available for both single user and multiuser environments.

Administration Module : It designed to create a

database of unlimited number of bibliographic records on all formats of library material. This module enables libraries in book acquisition and serial control. It facilitates pre-order searching of books, the orders against available books, generation of notices to the overdue and incomplete supplies, budget allocation and status of funds available under different heads, calculation of actual and committed expenses with appropriate currency conversions, generation of accession register etc.

Circulation Module : This module maintains and updates membership records. It checks the borrowers with their photo Identify through bar code scanning and prompts their loan status. It produces lists on loan, books due for return, facilitates reservation of titles, prompts overdue books, calculates fines and automatically generates notices to the borrowers.

OPAC : The data is fully protected from the users of OPAC terminals. The module facilitates members to search library material, based on Title, Author, Subject, Language, Key words, Accession Number, Publisher, Publishing Place and Year of Publication; supports bar code scanning, photo identity, and interface with Web internet besides generation of a number of reports Utilities Module facilitates the library staff to arrange the activities such as Binding, Photocopying, Translation etc. Report on work status, periodical reports on various activities can also be taken. Stock verification is possible through barcode scanner or manual entry. Web Inquiry allows access from the desktops to the Library and search for the Books, Articles and Journals. Demands for New Books/ Journals/Audio and Video equipment to library can also be submitted from desktops.

LibEra

LibEra is an integrated library software product from Modelsoft Ltd, Hyderabad. LibEra has been designed from the beginning to be web-enabled. It provides multi-lingual support. It is a comprehensive solution for all kinds of libraries. It covers all basic modules.

Its features include:

- It is platform independent; handles multiple libraries in an organization and virtual keyboards.
- Adheres to international standards like MARC21, AACR2R, ISO 2709 and 239.50 v1995.
- Multiple security; specific features are authorized to the members; provides high security for data.
- Library members are continuously sent information through automatic, system-generated e-mails
- Provision for usage of wild cards and keywords in enquiry.
- Maintains SDI profiles of the entire members and users are informed about new arrivals in the library through mails.
- Users can customize the look and feel of their screens.
- Client machines only need to have a browser to access the package.

Librarian Suite

Developed by Soft-Aid Computers Ltd, Pune, the software contains four subsystems, viz., Librarian for integrated library management functions; Librarian Q&A, Online Public Access Catalogue; Dossier for journal article indexing, archival and retrieval; and Librarian on Web for Internet/intranet ASP-based querying. The software is capable of working on DOS, UNIX and Windows platforms including Windows NT. It can handle more than 2 lakh records and is available in multi-lingual format. It can also handle user-defined media. It is installed in some R&D, banking and public sector institutions.

LibSys

It is a fully integrated library management system developed by LibSys Corporation, New Delhi. It is a multi-user system capable of running on DOS, UNIX, Xenix, VMS, and Windows platforms. It can be customized to suit the user needs and can be operated with other RDBMS software such as Ingress and Oracle. The LibSys 4 developed in C language is a client server implementation and provides ample flexibility in choosing operating platforms. It supports all UNIX, Windows NT, Novell NetWare environments and provides graphical user interface on client side. There are options for various MARC formats and CCF. It follows ANSI 2.39.50 protocol for bibliographic search. It can handle images and multimedia. Besides the library housekeeping operations, it supports article indexing, abstracts and generating CAS, SDI and bibliographies with full editing features. It has powerful search engine and Web interface for Internet/ intranet applications, options to have back-end RDBMS such as Oracle, or MS SQL.

Libraries of various public and private organizations, scientific laboratories, universities and colleges and public libraries in India use LibSys package. The LibSys software has been in operation since 1988. There are over 600 sites in different user segments throughout the country besides British Council Libraries (in South-Asian region) as well as a couple of Central American clients use the software. Many organizations have taken multiple site license of the software which includes British Council Libraries, Department of Space, CSIR, ICAR, Indian Oil Corporation, IIMs and IITs.

Acquisition Module covers initiation of titles for ordering with options to import data to download from network or enter data including checking for duplication; placing of orders; invoice processing; accessioning; order follow-up; receiving and accessioning of free and gift items are also dealt with online queries may be made on titles, orders, invoices, vendors, and budget heads; and corresponding reports can be printed. Various reports such as approval request form, purchase orders, overdue notices, budget and expenditure analysis, payment requisition report, accession register, and bill register can be generated and printed on requirement.

Cataloguing Module maintains a titles in-process file of all items that are accessioned. This system covers catalogue maintenance, thesaurus construction; authority files; and holdings updates. Holding summary by a range of call numbers and 3x5 catalog cards can be printed. It provides the facility to provide Current Awareness Services such as SDI, special bibliographies, and lists of recent arrivals. It makes possible import/export of bibliographic data in both MARC and non-March formats; and automates the stock verification process.

Circulation Module supports issue and returns, renewals, reservations and membership registration; generated and print barcoded ID Cards with the members photograph; titles on display; in circulation and in bindery; overdue follow-up and recall facility; inter-library loans and stock verification; Query and reports facilities cover a range of statistics on both borrowers and collection, including highly reserved titles, non-circulating material, number of check ins by title/borrower, delinquency cases, etc. The system keeps a complete log of all circulation transactions.

Serials Module provides for new subscription; renewal; invoice processing; budget & expenditure analysis (Kardex update); claims monitoring (including generating notices for issues 'not receiver', overdue, or received in a damaged condition); bindery management; recording and accessioning bound volumes; online queries on various aspects of serial control including the holdings and circulation of all periodicals.

OPAC provides access to the library holdings through

various catalogues and indexes such as author, title, subject, and classified catalogue, publishers' index, conference place index and KWIC/KWOC indexes. Also possible are combination searches using Boolean operators that yield highly satisfying and precise results, however complex the query. OPAC also provides the facility to request acquisition of titles, to reserve materials; and to send personalized SDI, overdue/recall/collect notices and messages by e-mail. Web OPAC provides and advanced GUI to enable searching of the library database through an industry standard web browser such as Netscape, Internet Explorer etc.

Article Indexing facilitates indexing and abstracting of articles from various journals in a separate database. It includes scanning of articles, entry of citation, online searches on author, keywords1descriptors and even word-based free text searches. This system also provides periodic documentation lists, personalized SDI, bibliographies on specific subjects, etc.

Maitrayee

Developed for use in the CALIBNET by the CMC Ltd, Secunderabad, Maitrayee facilitates library computerization, resource sharing, standardization, connectivity and modularity. The project was funded by NISSAT. It has been developed on Ingress RDBMS supported by UNIX platform. It is compatible with 180-2709 and conversion from CCF to UNIMARC or vice versa is possible. Other features like bar code reading and OCR are incorporated. Apart from routine library operations the software facilitates central host and networking services including supporting protocols like TCPIIP andX.25.

PALMS and CLMSZ

Prasad Automated Library Management Systems (PALMS) and Computerized Library Management Systems version 2 (CLMS2) are developed and distributed by the Nutan Software and Publishing, Almora. Both the software packages support most of the library routines and data conversions. They are Y2K complaint, compatible with dBase, FoxPro and word processing languages for report generation. PALMS also support CAS, SDI and bibliographical services. Both the packages are modestly priced and are within the reach of small and medium-sized libraries.

Sanjay

Sanjay is developed by DESIDOC and is marketed by NISSAT. This package is an extension of CDS/ISIS capabilities through the PASCAL interface. It has a set of 70 Pascal programs and 25special menus. It has a faster response time - 1 minute for a query on 12,000 documents. It interlinks effectively two or more databases and also handles numeric calculations. It is user-friendly for library housekeeping operations. Sanjay is based on CDS/ISIS ver. 2.3. It is capable of interlinking two or more databases, handling numerical calculations and other housekeeping operations.

The salient features of the package include Maintenance Module, User Module, Circulation Module and Online Catalogue Module. The Maintenance Module restricts the access rights as authorized by the Database Administrator. For data security and for providing selective access, the Maintenance Module is accessible to authorized users only. The User Module helps the library staff to carry out daily routine and assist the library users in circulation control, acquisition control, online catalogue and serials control. The Online Catalogue Module is interlinked to the circulation, acquisition and cataloguing activities. The major databases linked by it include books database, members database, acquisition database, vendors database, budget database and serials database. Any standard PC available nowadays can be used to run this software.

SLIM++

System for Library Information Management (SLIM) is a library software package from Algorithms, Pune. SLIM++ is an integrated, multi-user, multitasking library information software for the Windows environment. It helps the librarian catalogue books, firms, sound recordings, drawings, clippings, articles, reports, letters, pamphlets, serials publications etc. SLIM++ cataloguing adheres to popular international standards. One can share data with others effectively. Retrieval o f the data is simple, fast and efficient. It has Cataloguing, Circulation OPAC, Acquisition Serials Control, Web based OPAC, Bulletin Printing (CAS), Statistical Analysis, and Export/import in CCF/MARC, DBridge, 239.50server modules.

SLlM is widely used by many schools, colleges, research institutes, public libraries, corporate houses, etc. SLlM is upgraded continuously to meet the technological advances in the field of data storage, retrieval, user interaction and communications. SLIM++, highly revised version, has been introduced in May 2001. SLIM++ is user friendly, menu driven, and highly interactive software. To operate SLlM no prior knowledge of computers is required. On-site training and high quality reference manuals ensure smooth transition from the current computerized or manual system to SLIM (Vyasamurthy, 2001).

General Features

- Minimal data entry, pick-up lists during data entry, validation and integrity checks.
- Bar code support with multimedia links.
- Browsing your library information through the Internet/Intranet.
- Multi-script/multi-fonts.
- Variable length fields records, packing purging records.
- Existing data conversion to SLIM++.

- Optional customized retrospective data entry and data capture.
- Multiple selection criteria for reports.
- Windows Features.
- Adherence to Windows standards with menu bar, taskbar, window resizing, window moving, multi tasking using simultaneous operations in multiple windows.
- Point and click reduces user's learning curve.
- Drag and drop, cut and paste reduce data entry efforts and increases uniformity and accuracy of the data.
- Wizard mode for beginners; to formulate search query, users need not remember steps.
- Online help /tool tips.
- Use of Windows standards dialogues for saving, opening and search in.
- Use of rich text format for user specified fonts, colors and sizes.
- Multi-media links to drawings, sounds, scanned files, web sites etc.
- Interface with standards Windows applications like Wordpad, MS-Word, Mail Exchangers, etc.

SOUL

University libraries are complex entities, having large collections and serving a huge clientele. To carry out various operations in a university library effectively, there is a need for automation. Keeping in view the latest trends in information technology, INFLIBNET Center has developed a Windows-based library management software SOUL (Software for University Libraries), which provides total solution for library automation. SOUL is designed using client-server architecture, which imparts extra strength to storage capacity, multiple accesses to single database, various levels of security, back up, and storage facilities etc. This software has been designed after a comprehensive study of different library-related functions practiced in university libraries. It has MS-SQL Server 6.5 RDBMS as the back end. This user-friendly software is quite easy to work with. The software comprises Acquisition, Catalogue, Circulation, OPAC, Serial Control, and Administration modules.

The in-built network feature of the software will allow multiple libraries of the same university to function together as well as access to the distributed databases installed at various university libraries and union catalogue mounted at INFLIBNET using VSAT network. Other features include availability at nominal cost to university libraries, software designed and developed exclusively to work under university environment, network feature of the software will allow multiple libraries of university to function together, exhaustive training at INFLIBNET supported by comprehensive manual, on-site training and free updating/modification, free technical assistance and following standard formats such as CCF, AACR2, and LCSH.

Suchika

It is an integrated software package, exclusively developed by DESIDOC for use by the Defence Science Library (of DESIDOC) and other libraries technical information centers of the Defence R&D Organization (DRDO). One of the objectives was to follow uniform standards for creating Holdings Database of DRDO Libraries and to help automate the DRDO libraries. Initially, Suchika was developed in C++ language on MS-DOS and UNIX, and version 2 on Windows NT platform. The software conforms the CCF, AACRZ and 180-2709 and allows data conversion from CDS/ISIS, dBase and FoxPro through application programmes. It is Y2K complaint.

The software has powerful search facilities. Suchika version 2 offers many new facilities over the previous version. Apart from Y2K compliance and supporting all library routines, the software has capabilities to interface with Web internet. One can search the OPAC, which is hosted on the Web, and download information. Alternatively, DESIDOC can send downloaded files (against a query) through email, which is provided for in Suchika version 2. Another unique feature is adding titles and abstracts of serials received to generate CAS, SDI, Current Additions (books and periodicals) and generating catalogue of bound volumes (for individual libraries) or union catalogue (for a group of libraries). The databases can be converted to CD-ROM. It facilitates duplicate checking also. Comtek Computers Pvt.Ltd., the developer (for DESIDOC) of Suchika, markets a variant of this software under the trade name Troodon.

Virtua ILS

Virtua Integrated Library System is a comprehensive, integrated library software package from VTLS Inc, Virginia, and USA. It has the modules of Acquisition and Fund Management, Circulation, Cataloging, Serials Control etc. There are several features that are unique to VTLS Virtua ILS (Vyasamurthy, 2001).

- It is fully parameterized software: User library can configure the setting to its maximum flexibility.
- It adopts UNICODE and as a result can support number of language fonts not normally supported by others.
- ILS has 239.0 built into the software. As a result, ILS users can reach external library catalogs easily and conduct searches. Converse is also true, if other libraries permit access to reach external databases. [For information on 239.50.
- There is a powerful language editor to input records in different languages.

- It has provision for RFID tags and labels (see note below on RFID)
- It comes with a Chameleon Gateway: With the help of this gateway, the user's screen can be customized according to his needs.
- It has an exhaustive statistics and reporting module.

It comes with heavy security possibilities: Security of access can be monitored at user, user Group, patron, and patron group and location library levels. Depending upon security rights granted to you, the tool bar on your screen contains only those icons that are usable by you.

A Note on RFID Technology: RFID stands for Radio Frequency Identification. Labels, which are as thin as paper, contain electronic chip, embedded with details of the patron, accession number of a book etc. These are pasted onto books, user's cards etc. RFID sensing devices 'read' these RFID labels or Tags remotely from a distance, that is, no line of sight positioning of the reader is needed. As a result, a number of advantages arise.

Stock verification and inventory control could be carried out using hand held reading devices. Just wave the reader across the shelf, all accession numbers are read in.

- Theft detection is possible if a reader is fitted to the exit door. When a user unauthorized takes out a book, RFID scanner detects it and raises an alarm.
- Unmanned self-service counters can be maintained for checking in and checking out books. After scanning incoming books, software automatically "cancels" the issue.
- Identification of misplaced items will become easy.
- Greater availability of books because wrong shelving can be avoided and corrected.
- It leads to greater efficiency and productivity in library.

- New Hanovar County Public Library in North Carolina has started using RFID technology from January 2001. In Hyderabad, the Central University of Hyderabad has procured Virtua ILS for automating their Digital Library.

1.6. EVALUATION, TRENDS AND FUTURE OF LIBRARY AUTOMATION SOFTWARE

The selection of library management software is a complex and time consuming one. Apart from thorough knowledge of library system, sub-systems, procedures, activities and tasks, it requires the knowledge of LMSs features and trends in the development of ICT. The selection process should be based on seven basic steps – evaluation, comparison, demonstration of package, feedback from authority, staff and users, preliminary selection, modification and customisation and final selection. The process of evaluation should be based on some predefined criteria. Now we will study the essential criteria for evaluation, recent trends and future directions of library automation software packages.

1.6.1. Criteria for Evaluation

The following factors should be taken into consideration at the time of evaluation of any library automation package:

- Vendor Validity
- Services Availability Checklist
- Core services
- Enhanced services
- Value-added services
- Functional Checklist
- Data Conversion and Backup Utility
- Training, Documentation and Customer Support
- Hardware and Third Party Software Requirements
- Performance Testing

1.6.2. Trends and Future

The rapid developments of ICT have changed the libraries over the last few decades. The library systems all over the world are going through a process of transformation to address the effects and implications of technological change. In response to the needs of the hour, library automation packages are gradually being upgraded to satisfy diversified demands of library authority, staff and users by incorporating various epoch-making features. Some of these features are selected for discussion here on the basis of their importance and utilities in library management.

- Unicode
- Z39.50 Information Retrieval Protocol
- Web-centric Architecture
- Integrated Access Interface
- FRBR based Bibliographic Data Model
- Interoperability and Crosswalk
- RFID and Smart Card Based Inventory Control
- Open Source Software

1.7. SUMMARY

Library automation encompasses mechanisation of housekeeping operations, sophisticated information retrieval, integrated access interface and MIS activities. The process of library automation centers on automation package or library management software. Modern packages are integrated in nature and offer all the facilities essential for day-to-day library management. Automation packages available in India are basically of three types – packages of foreign origin, packages developed over foreign LMSs and packages developed in India. These packages are modular in structure and most of them supports all the housekeeping operations, OPAC, Web-OPAC, digital media archiving, Z39.50 copy cataloguing and modern data capture devices like RFID, smartcard, etc. The process of selection of LMS should be based on some well defined criteria because implementation of LMS is a big investment in terms of money, time and manpower.

REVIEW QUESTIONS

1. Describe the History and Development of Library Automation?
2. Explain the Development of Library Automation Software in India?
3. List Trends and Future of Library Automation Software?

2

Acquisition and Cataloguing

STRUCTURE

2.0. OBJECTIVES

- To find out the methods used for training of library staff and users
- To identify the limitations of acquisition and cataloguing in Library
- To discover the methods used for user awareness and access to Library
- To identify the strategy used in preservation of Library
- To identify the various users services using cataloguing module
- To find out the concept of shared cataloguing and OPAC

2.1. INTRODUCTION

Most of the procedures related to library housekeeping operations are interlinked with each other in a coherent manner. The relationship between the procedures under acquisition subsystem and the tasks related to cataloguing procedure under processing subsystem is quite obvious. In an acquisition module of any Library Management Software (LMS), we have to enter administrative, financial and bibliographical data related to the documents to be procured in libraries. An integrated library management system will transfer necessary bibliographic data (such as author, title, and edition) of newly procured documents to the cataloguing module of the package as and when those are marked received in the acquisition module. It saves unnecessary duplication of data or data redundancy and thereby achieves economy in terms of time, manpower and money. As a result, acquisition and cataloguing are now placed under a common module in library automation packages. For example in SOUL acquisition and cataloguing are two separate modules but KOHA (a recently developed automation package) treats these two processes under the same module called acquisition. Cataloguing of existing library resources is done through the sub-module "Retrospective Conversion" under catalogue module of automation packages.

2.2. COMPUTERISED ACQUISITION SUBSYSTEM

The basic activities of any computerised ordering or acquisition subsystem can be specified as follows:

- To receive indents/suggestions for the documents to be acquired
- To check whether items requested are already in the library or on order
- To obtain approval of the competent authorities for purchase of the indented/suggested documents
- To print orders or dispatch order electronically to supplier/publishers
- To check when orders are overdue
- To follow up overdue orders
- To maintain a file of records of items on order
- To note the arrival of ordered items
- To process bills for payment
- To maintain book fund statistics and accounts
- To generate printed and electronic listing of various reports
- To control currency conversions
- To maintain vendor performance reports and statistics

The acquisition module of modern Library Management Software (LMS) should also carry out the following jobs.

Accommodate a variety of materials, including but not limited to – monographs, monograph series, annual and cumulative indexes, loose leaf materials, supplements, reports, musical scores etc.

Accommodate and identify items in a variety of formats, including but not limited to – print, microform, film, videotape, audio cassette, CD-ROM, magnetic tape, etc.

Record, store and display - bibliographic information, acquisition type (order, gift, approval etc.), status (reported, received, etc.), library/branch/copy/fund information, invoice information, vendor information, accounting information, requestor information etc.

Accommodate different types of orders – regular order, membership, approval, standing (continuing) order, deposit account etc.

2.2.1. Acquisition Work

The acquisition work includes the functions that facilitate a library to procure and process new books from different sources. Document can be procured either through request from a member or books sent by vendors/ suppliers on approval. The bibliographic details (available from request form or books themselves) provide maximum information to place orders.

Group I tasks : The work of this group starts with entering bibliographical information and information about requestors from the suggestion slips and books submitted by the suppliers on approval. Bibliographical data given by the requestors in suggestion slips should be verified by consulting book selection tools. The online databases of virtual bookstores on the World Wide Web (WWW) may also be utilised for checking bibliographical information of recently published documents. Bibliographical details of documents received by libraries in excretes are also entered into the database. A library normally receives a large number of suggestions and documents for ordering. The library staff short lists these requests depending on need, availability of fund etc. by clicking the appropriate option(s) available in the package. Finally a report is generated for all the short-listed suggestions and documents indicating number of copies required, budget code, budget head and unit price of the items requested. The library committee approves the list officially and on the basis of the final approval list, library staff either selects or reject the short listed titles. Books on direct approval and gratis items do not have to go through approval process from library committee or any such authoritative body.

Group II tasks : The first step of this group is to select listed vendors (available from master files) for placing orders of approved documents. Order letters are then printed as per the format created in the pre-acquisition stage indicating name of supplier with address, reference number, terms and conditions and expected date of delivery etc. This group also includes the tasks of reordering, reminder generation (for a particular order or to a particular supplier/publisher) and report generation (for ordered items, overdue orders, budget commitment etc.).

Group III tasks : This group the works of receiving and accessioning of ordered documents. In case of barcode based circulation system, barcode labels for accessioned items are also generated in this sub-module of the package. The requestor or department may be informed about the arrival of requested documents in the library by generating intimation letter from the package.

Group IV tasks : The work of this group starts with the processing of invoices received from the suppliers along with the documents by entering necessary elements into the database. Release of payment is the next step in which letters/reports containing all the necessary administrative and financial details are generated against supplier or order number or invoice number for requesting appropriate authority (generally Finance Section) to release payment to the supplier. After release of payment, the financial details of payment are entered and stored into the database.

2.2.2. Output of Computerised Acquisition Subsystem:

- The outputs form a computerised acquisition subsystem usually include the following:List/Report of item(s) requested
- List/Report of item(s) from supplier/publisher
- Item(s) selected for approval
- Item(s) approved by the authority/library committee
- Item(s) rejected in the approval process
- List of gratis item(s) received by library
- Report on request status
- Printout or soft copy of letters for approval
- Printout or soft copy of order letters and query letters
- Printout or soft copy of reminder letters
- Printout or soft copy of order cancellation letters
- Printout or soft copy of reordering
- Letters for adjustment of advance payments
- Letters to bank for foreign exchange rate
- Report on order status
- List/Report of item(s) selected for order
- List/Report of overdue item
- List/Report of item(s) actually ordered
- Reports of budget commitment
- List/Report of item ordered against advance payment
- List/Report of item(s) received against orders
- Letters of intimation (on arrival of documents)
- Printout of accession register
- Printout of barcode labels
- List of supplier/publishers
- List of currency and exchange rates Acquisition and Cataloguing

— Budget with commitments
— Report of detailed annual budget of library
— Report of amount received in different budget heads
— Report/statistics of vendor performance
— List of recent additions
— Generation of book cards (in case of integrated ordering and cataloguing system)

2.2.3. Problems in Acquisition

Acquisition work is not an easy task. It has got its own problems. Some are common to libraries everywhere while some are peculiar to India. Major problems are brought out in the section so that you can be prepared to face them. They are:

- Conflicting factors of demand, supply and finance;
- The situation created by far-off book markets;
- The difficulties in dealing with local book suppliers;
- The problems relating to foreign publications;
- The special problems concerning Indian publications;
- Publications needing pre-paid orders; and
- The question of out-of-print and rare books.

2.2.4. Acquisition Department

Libraries are organised into units / departments / sections based on the functions that they are expected to perform. Acquisition Department (AD) is one among them and is concerned with various activities relating to collection development. Its objective is to build up information resources in conformity with the objectives of the parent institution on the one hand, and that which is suitable to the differential information requirements of the different users on the other. It involves the processes of selection, procurement and accessioning of documents.

The requirements of selection and acquisition are given below:

Selection Requires : A Selection Policy (involving a statement about users and needs; subject, topic or mission to be dealt with and type of information sources to be covered). Selection Aids and Tools which will help in selection and verification. Specification of a Selection Process (involving decisions on who selects; procedures for judging intrinsic value of information in sources and procedures for judging demand and user appropriateness).

Acquisition/Procurement Requires : Procedures for procurement of necessary information sources. In cases where no outright procurement is planned or possible procedures for access to sources, e.g. getting on loan, photocopying pertinent sections, getting permission to use them in another information centre/ system etc. have to be set.

Accessioning Requires : Specification of procedures for taking all the books and documents acquired to be added to the stock of the library which involves the assignment of a serial number called Accession Number and, if applicable, a Donation Number. Every item and its bibliographic details thus, entered in the Accession Register.

Thus, these three successive stages of operations - selection; procurement and accessioning - correspond to the three sections of the Acquisition Department. The collection of a library, as you know, can contain various types of documents. Some libraries may have a special preference for specific types of documents. However, in most libraries books form the major part of the collection. It is, therefore, usual to refer to the activities in AD as book selection, book ordering and book accessioning respectively. Nevertheless, it may be noted that acquisition of all types of documents comes within the scope of AD. However, there is one exception. Acquiring current issues of periodicals and newspapers in not done by AD. Instead it is done by the Periodicals Department. AD has to deal with periodicals and newspapers only when they are received as bound volumes.

AD has a very crucial place in the overall organisation of a library. Its importance lies in the fact that collection is the basic factor in the usefulness of a library and that collection development is primarily the task of this department. AD, therefore, must organise tile resources made available to it (men, materials and money) in such a way as to facilitate the building lip of the collection in the most efficient and economic way. The fulfillment of this task involves all the basic elements and sound principles of scientific management.

Acquisitions Procedures : Acquisitions procedures should describe all steps from initial screening to final selection. It is important to list the type of materials that are collected, why they are needed, and how they are obtained.

In addition to selection of new resources, policies on re-evaluation (weeding), replacing and repairing materials, and gift materials may also be included. The specific procedures for acquiring material for a library's collection will vary between library types and individual libraries. Patron recommendations for acquisitions are often encouraged in all library types. Selectors are responsible for reading reviews and staying informed about current trends in purchasing, and the library's professional staff is responsible for making the final decisions about acquiring material.

Acquisitions Procedures in Public Libraries : Ideally, in larger public libraries, multiple members of a library's staff are responsible for reviewing material for purchase. The selection policy will outline the specific areas in which a library collects materials. Those areas should be identified and selectors should be assigned for the identified collection areas. In a smaller library, one person may be responsible for selecting resources.

Example: Public Library Acquisitions Procedures

The public library has a number of selectors on the staff, each responsible for a different level of collection development:

The general manager of the main library and the general manager of branches and mobile services have the system-wide responsibility for the overall selection and maintenance of all materials and formats within the collection of the library. This responsibility is monitored by the library director and assistant director, and is delegated to these individuals as a result of their education, training, experience, and job classification.

All materials and formats are selected or approved for the library's collection by a main library division manager, or by staff members within that division, who are qualified to do so by reason of education, training, experience, knowledge of subject area, and job classification.

Approved materials can be selected for the various collections within each branch library or mobile services unit by the branch library manager, mobile services manager, or other agency staff who are qualified to do so by reason of education, training, experience, or job classification.

Acquisitions Procedures in School Libraries : Because most school libraries have only a single school librarian, that individual is responsible for creating a collection to support instruction, literacy, and student's recreational reading. Materials selection policies generally mandate that the library professional seek input from teachers, other professional staff, and students. School librarians are also responsible for weeding or de-selecting collection materials following policy guidelines as well as making a decision as to whether gift items will be accepted.

Example: School Library Acquisitions Procedures

In selecting learning resources, professional personnel will evaluate available resources and curriculum needs and will consult reputable, professionally prepared aids to selection, and other appropriate sources. The actual resource will be examined whenever possible.

Recommendations for purchase involve administrators, teachers, students, district personnel, and community members, as appropriate.

Gift materials shall be judged by the selection criteria and shall be accepted or rejected by those criteria.

Selection is an ongoing process that should include removing materials that are no longer used or needed, adding materials, and replacing lost and worn materials that still have educational value.

Acquisition Procedures in Academic Libraries : Ideally, multiple members of a library's staff are responsible for reviewing material for purchase. The selection policy should outline the specific areas in which a library will collect, and professional library staff members should be assigned to select material for specific collection areas. Librarians may consult and get input from faculty about purchase, but the final acquisition decisions are the responsibility of the appointed librarian or librarians.

Example: Academic Library Acquisition Procedures

Item selection is done by professional librarians (selectors) with support from the faculty. Each selector is responsible for recommending material for purchase in their assigned subject areas. Selectors may work with their respective faculty members to identify material and make purchasing decisions that best meet the curriculum goals.

2.3. COMPUTERISED CATALOGUING SUBSYSTEM

Automated cataloguing systems are useful to control the clerical and technical processes involved, and to promote the exchange and use of cataloguing data locally, regionally, nationally and globally. Over the last 20 years, databases and Online Public Access Cataloguing (OPAC) have gradually replaced card, sheaf and microform catalogues. The catalogue records have become the central bibliographic record for the exchange management system. A computerised catalogue record requires to be standardised for the interchange of cataloguing records. Standardisation and structuring of cataloguing records are based on content designators such as MARC 21 (Machine Readable Cataloguing), CCF (Common Communication Format), UNIMARC (Universal MARC)or other similar standards.

2.3.1. Basic Requirements for Catalogue Module

In view of the recent developments in ICT sector, a modern LMS should provide appropriate facilities in its catalogue module. The basic necessities of the module for machine-readable cataloguing may be formulated as follows:

(a) Bibliographic Requirements : Should support a variety of classification schemes and vocabulary control devices (e.g. subject headings lists or thesauri and electronic resource description formats)

- Must enable coverage of standard bibliographic and authority record formats (e.g. MARC, CCF etc.)
- Must enable records to be exported or imported to and from tape, disk or other devices
- Must enable a bibliographic record to be retrieved and modified at any time, once it has been entered
- Must enable coverage of items like monographs, serials, government documents or any other type of documents
- Must enable catalogue data to be added, validated, updated and removed online from the workstations
- Must support withdrawal of items, export and import of records

(b) Authority Control Requirements

- Must enable incorporating changes in the MARC authority format or other national/international standard formats
- Must generate various kinds of references from authority records
- Must accommodate:
- Personal, corporate and topical names headings in a name authority file
- Title, uniform title, and series entries in a title authority file
- Subject headings in a subject authority file

(c) OPAC Requirements : The LMS should facilitate the following functionalities with record to OPAC/Web OPAC:

- Must allow both simple and expert searching
- Must support users to enter multiple words or phrases to be searched on one , more than one or all fields
- Should support Boolean operators, within and across all fields, such as:
- OR (either one or both terms must be in the record)
- XOR (either term, but not both, must be in the record)
- AND (both terms must be in the same record)
- NOT (following term must not appear in any record)
- Should support positional operators
- SAME (terms must be in the same field)
- WITH (terms must be in the same sentence within a field)
- NEAR (terms must be adjacent to one another, but in either order)
- ADJ (terms must be immediately adjacent to one another)

- Should support relational operators (less than, greater than, equal to, etc.)
- Should include user self-service features such as reservation of items, cancellation of reserved items.
- Must enable users to limit searches by: publication year, language, item type, item category, location and access
- Must support multilingual features
- Must enable searchers to specify which fields are to be displayed and to indicate brief or full display of hits

(d) Downloading Requirements

- Must be Z39.50 compliant cataloguing system [ANSI/NISO Z39.50 (1995) or ISO239.50 (1998)]
- Should enable to capture bibliographic and authority records from any Z39.50 server through Z39.50 client
- Should allow local manipulation of captured data.

(e) Reports and Backup Requirements

- Must produce a count of all records added, edited by a specific operator or over a specified time period
- Must generate lists, statistics of items added or tabulated by call number, document type, adjustment location etc.
- Must produce a list of all citations with authority file violations
- Must support backup of all cataloguing records in suitable media (magnetic, optical etc.) and easy recovery of records at the time of need.

2.3.2. Computerised Cataloguing Jobs

The process of computerised catalogues usually covers the following jobs:

(a) Titles in Process : These are the documents,

which have been received from the suppliers and technical processing.

(b) Retrospective Conversion : This involves preparation of machine-readable catalogue of old and existing library stock. Here the cataloguing data is first entered on a worksheet or datasheet designed by following any standard content designator scheme and then data transferred to the database through manual keying. However, if the cataloguers have enough experience catalogue entries can be directly keyed into the system as per a standard input format.

(c) Existing Library Catalogue in Machine-Readable Form : Development of library OPAC started long back in many libraries of the world and at that time integrated library automation packages were not available. As a result, cataloguing data in digital format are available in many libraries, which can be merged into the catalogue database created using the newly installed LMS.

(d) Union Catalogue : Union files of the stock of several libraries, or another shared database may be imported, converted into local standard format and finally merged into the catalogue database.

(e) Commercially Available Files of MARC Records: In this process records from external databases may be downloaded directly from the relevant websites or CD-ROMS.

- Basic Jobs in Cataloguing
- The key jobs of a cataloguing module are:
- Authority control
- Data entry
- For newly acquired document
- For existing old stock
- Downloading

These jobs should also be supplemented by regular backup of the catalogue database in suitable media. In the family of magnetic storage devices, Digital Audio Tape (DAT) is the most popular in libraries all over the world. DVD-ROM – an optical storage device with a typical storage capacity of 17 GB is coming a big way to replace all other backup media for the storage of library records.

(a) Authority File Creation and Maintenance : Authority file is essential to control form of index terms or headings, such as author headings, or subject index terms for better retrieval efficiency. Records in this file maybe created locally or drawn from externally available files such as the name and subject authority files of the Library of Congress or other agencies. Alternatively, one or more suitable thesauri may be used to build up the authority file. Library automation packages provide a facility to create and maintain authority file in the catalogue module. This file acts as a master database, where entry is to be made once. This gets reflected in various modules of the package. The master file containing authority entries can be consulted during cataloguing, possibly by display in a separate window and new headings are immediately added to the authority file with an opportunity to review subsequently.

(b) Data Entry for Cataloguing : This facility of the catalogue module is utilized for generating bibliographic data elements to the newly acquired documents and also for entering bibliographical data of existing old stock of the library. An integrated automation package uses the bibliographical details created for the acquisition module for the catalogue module also. In the catalogue module the record is standardized by entering additional data elements and rendering of access points with the help of authority file. The transformation of bibliographical data elements of existing stock of any library into machine-readable form is called Retrospective Conversion or simply RECON.

(c) Copy Cataloguing and Downloading : In this process, cataloguing as particular document, the cataloguing data is downloaded from an external OPAC and necessary changes in some fields like those of accession numbers, keywords, etc, are made. This approach helps in reducing cataloguing. The OPAC of US Library Congress is perhaps the best source for downloading bibliographic data pertaining to books. For other types of documents like reports, research papers, etc. relevant databases may have to be accessed. This mode of shared cataloguing is popularly termed as copy cataloguing.

Advantages of Automated Cataloguing

There are several advantages of automated cataloguing. A well designed automated cataloguing system should have the following functions and advantages:

- Creation of a record for a document only once;
- No main or added entries of catalogue are necessary;
- Any field may be .made searchable;
- Composite and interactive searches extend versatility;
- Outputs can be obtained in any desired format;
- Data input and retrieval is much faster;
- Repetitive work is eliminated;
- Import/export of bibliographic data is possible; and
- Interlinking with external databases is possible.

2.3.3. Features of Automated Cataloguing

Catalogue module is used for retrospective conversion of library resources. It also facilitates library staff to process the newly acquired library resources. The important features of catalogue module are:

- UNICODE-based multilingual support for Indian and foreign languages;
- Compliant to International Standards such as

MARC21, AACR-2, MARCXML;

- Supports multi-platform for bibliographic database such as My SQL, MS- SQL or any other RDBMS;
- Supports cataloguing of electronic resources such as e-journals, e-books, virtually any type of material;
- Supports online copy cataloguing from MARC21 bibliographic database;
- Provides default templates for data entry of different type of documents. User can also customize their own data entry templates for different type of documents;
- Provides freedom to users for generating reports of their choice and format along with template and query parameters;
- Provides facility to send reports through e-mail, allows users to save the reports in various formats such as PDF, Excel, MARCXML, etc. ;
- Highly versatile and user-friendly OPAC with simple and advanced search. OPAC users can export their search results into PDF, MS Excel, and MARCXML format;
- Supports authority files of personal name and corporate body;
- Supports data exchange through ISO-2709 standard;
- Global Search and replace a word or a phrase;
- Different templates for leaders and fixed fields of MARC21;
- Allows user-generated customized reports;
- Facilitates authority database of person name, corporate body, subject headings and series name; and
- Supports copy cataloguing in MARC21 format by using ISO- 2709 standard.

Creation and Maintenance of Authority File

Modern ILMSs are based on relational data model. Each module of these packages centers on a master database. Any number of additions, modifications and deletions are possible in the master database and these changes are automatically reflected in all the sub-modules of the catalogue. Cataloguing module also follows architecture, wherein records created in the master database are available to all the sub-modules. It reduces data entry work and ensures standardization. Generally, master database is the database where entry is to be made once that gets reflected thought out its various sub modules.

Authority file is essential to index terms or headings, such as author headings, or subject index terms for better retrieval efficiency. Records in this file may be created locally or drawn from externally available files such as the name and subject authority files of the Library of Congress or other agencies. Alternatively, one or more suitable thesauri may be used to build up the authority file. Library automation packages provide a facility to create and maintain authority file in the catalogue module. This acts as a master database, where entry is to be made once. This gets reflected in various modules of the package. The master file containing authority entries can be consulted during cataloguing, possibly by display in a separate window and new headings are immediately added to the authority file with an opportunity to review subsequently. The following are the master databases:

Name : In this file, provides authoritative data for names of persons, organizations, events, places, and titles. Its purpose is the identification of these entities and, through the use of such controlled vocabulary, to provide uniform access to bibliographic resources. Names descriptions also provide access to a controlled form of name through references from unused forms. Names may also be used as subjects in bibliographic descriptions; it may be combined with controlled values from subject heading schemes, such as LCSH.

Publisher : This master file contains contact details of all local and foreign publishers who have publishing books and serials along with their corresponding codes. These codes are generally created locally.

Subject : These master files holds lists of subject descriptors and are available in various sub-modules for entering subject headings for books and serials. This master also includes class numbers, corresponding to subjects covered.

Country : This file contains names of countries and their corresponding codes for entering details of country of publication in sub-modules of cataloguing module, The Country code is generally based on ISO-3166 where each country is represented by two unique characters e.g. the code for India is as per ISO-3166 standards.

Language : This file contains entries for languages and their three digit codes as per the ISDS manual.

Physical Media Type : Library materials are available in different types of media which are defined in master file. These physical media can be selected for creation of bibliographic record. The physical media will help user to navigate required title in different forms of resources. It may be textual document, CD-ROM, magnetic tape, online, DVD-ROM, etc. This file includes description and corresponding codes for different physical media.

Corporate Body : This master file contains contact details of corporate bodies that have publishing books and serials along with their corresponding codes.

Meeting : The master file contains name of the meeting, date, place where it has been taken. The most of the options are similar with corporate body.

Series : The master file contains name of the series under which various publication are brought out.

2.3.4. Process of Computerised Catalogues

Titles in Process : The titles, which have been entered in the acquisition module, will appear under this option in the cataloguing module. It allows to feed the missing information accurately, correct the details like title/author, edition, publisher, place, year, subjected headings, keywords, physical description, etc. if required. Feed local holding information such as shelving location, collection type (Lending, Reference, and Special), classification number, book number, accession number and other relevant information about the title from the physical book or from other sources.

Retrospective Conversion : There are a number of options for retro conversion as mentioned below :

(i) ***Manual*** **:** The majority of the libraries are creating bibliographical records in the database through manual keying by using various data sources such as data input sheets, accession register, catalogue cards. In the catalogue module the record is standardized by entering additional data elements and rendering of access points with the help of authority file.

(ii) ***Existing library catalogue*** **:** Development of library OPAC started long back in many libraries of the world and at that time Integrated Library Automation Packages were not available. As such, cataloguing data available in digital format can be merged into the catalogue database created using the newly installed ILMS.

(iii) ***Union Catalogue*** **:** Union database is unified Online Library Catalogues of books, theses and journals of the participating libraries It contains bibliographic description, location and holdings information of the books, journals and theses, etc. It is a major source of bibliographic information that can be used for inter-library loan, collections development as well as for copy cataloguing and retro-conversion of bibliographic records.

(iv) ***Commercially available files of MARC records*** : Records from external databases may be downloaded directly from the relevant online databases such as OCLC or CD-ROM databases.

(v) ***Other Sources*** : Copy cataloguing denotes the process of downloading bibliographic records from cataloguing utilities or vendor online systems. This is the most popular method in many libraries. Creating complete, new bibliographic records from scratch is known as original cataloguing. Many libraries download bibliographic records directly to local online catalogues from bibliographic databases such as OCLC, INFLIBNET's IndCat, a commercial vendor database, or other library's online catalogues.

Import/Export : Data import/export facility is available in most of the ILMS software, which allows to:

- Import MARC records (data downloaded from various sites/files obtained from the
- Publishers, LOC, IndCat, etc.) to ILMS software
- Export ILMS records into MARC21 format
- Convert CCF (Common Communication Format) records into MARC format
- Import MARCXML data into ILMS software and
- Provision to add accession numbers to imported data.

2.4. STANDARDS FOR BIBLIOGRAPHIC FORMATS

MARC

Several options are available for libraries for automating cataloguing activities; the most widely used method is by using MARC format. It is to the credit of Library of Congress for having recognized the need for developing a record structure and format which would greatly facilitate the exchange of bibliographic information between libraries, group of libraries and computer systems. Early trials around 1966 worked with MARC I format, and superseded in 1967 by MARC II often referred as MARC. Presently, most of the ILMS software are using MACR21.

"MARC format" is a widely accepted structural coding scheme for a particular type of material, including monographs, serials, sound recordings, scores, manuscripts, maps, audio-visual materials, and machine readable data files. The data that can be included in a MARC format include almost all information represented on cataloguing cards such as author, title editor, physical description, series statement, notes, subject headings, added entries call number and various control numbers plus a great deal of other information which is helpful for categorization and processing by the computer.

CCF (Common Communication Format)

UNESCO's General Information Programme (PGI) recommended MARC format for libraries and UNSISIT Reference Manual for abstracting and indexing agencies. But, because it is common for developing countries to support only a single bibliographic agency, some countries have indicated that they find neither of these two formats entirely satisfactory. The direct result of this dissatisfaction has been the development of Common Communication Format (CCF). It was first published by UNESCO in 1984. It provides a standard for bibliographic records in machine readable form that will be useful for both library and non-library agencies. It follows the rules for bibliographic record formats laid down in ISO.

UNIMARC

MARC formats were also developed in other countries like Canada, Latin America, Spain, Denmark, Australia, Japan, Germany, France, Belgium, Switzerland, etc. The multiplicity of these formats made it difficult to exchange machine readable data on an international scale. The IFLA Working Group on Content Designators formed in 1973 under the joint auspices of the Committee on Cataloguing and Committee on Mechanization took steps to establish what is known as 'UNIMARC', which could facilitate translation of records and international exchange of data.

The basics of 'UNIMARC' are ISBD with full content designation provided for full data elements. The primary purpose of UNIMARC was to facilitate the international exchange of bibliographic data in machine-readable form between national bibliographic agencies. UNIMARC may also be used as a model for the development of new machine-readable bibliographic formats.

The scope of UNIMARC was to specify the content designators (tags, indicators Automation of Cataloguing and subfield codes) to be assigned to bibliographic records in machine-readable form and to specify the logical and physical format of the records. It covers monographs, serials, cartographic materials, music, sound recordings, graphics, projected and video materials, rare books and electronic resources.

UNIMARC was intended to be a carrier format for exchange purposes. It does not stipulate the form, content, or record structure of the data within individual systems. Records are usually structured in exchange tape format as the last stage in any conversion process after form, content, and content designators have been converted to the UNIMARC standard. Those organizations intending to use UNIMARC for data interchange will find it useful to co-ordinate their internal format content designators and field and sub field definitions with those in UNIMARC to reduce the complexity of data conversion when the records are converted into the UNIMARC exchange tape structure.

ISBD

International Standard Bibliographic Description (ISBD) was developed out of a resolution of the International Meeting of Cataloguing Experts, organized by the IFLA Committee on Cataloguing in Copenhagen in 1969, which recommended that standardization of the form and content of bibliographic description be established. This ISBD contained provisions covering machine readable data files. However, when the ISBD (NBM) was being reviewed, together with the ISBD (CM), ISBD (M), and ISBD(S), by the ISBD Review Committee formed by IFLA in 1981, it was decided that special consideration should be given to the rapidly increasing need for a separate ISBD for computer files. With the development of programs and data files for smaller computers, the ISBD (CF) was published in 1988 as a result of developments like emergence of interactive multimedia, development of optical technology availability of remote electronic resources on the Internet and World Wide Web, and reproductions of electronic resources. These formats conform to AACR2 Rules and are also useful for exchange of bibliographic data.

2.4.1. Functional Requirements for Bibliographic Records (FRBR)

Functional Requirements for Bibliographic Records (FRBR) is a conceptual entity-relationship model developed by the International Federation of Library Associations and Institutions (IFLA) to describe entities, relationships, and attributes (i.e., metadata). User tasks of retrieval and access in online library catalogues and bibliographic databases from a user's perspective. It represents a more holistic approach to retrieval and access as the relationships between the entities provide links to navigate through the hierarchy of relationships. The model is significant because it is separate from specific cataloguing standards such as AACR2 or International

Standard Bibliographic Description (ISBD).

The Functional Requirements for Bibliographic Records – the entities, relationships, and attributes from that model to describe how it is currently affecting work on the Anglo-American Cataloguing Rules and the extension of the model into the area of authority control.

Resource Description and Access (RDA)

Resource Description and Access (RDA) is a standard for cataloguing that provides instructions and guidelines on formulating bibliographic data. Intended for use by libraries and other cultural organizations such as museums and archives, RDA is the successor to the Anglo-American Cataloguing Rules, Second Edition (AACR2), the current cataloging standard set for English language libraries. RDA was initially released in June 2010.

The primary distinction between RDA and AACR is structural. RDA is organised based on the Functional Requirements for Bibliographic Records (FRBR). These principles identify both the 'user tasks' which a library catalogue should make possible and a hierarchy of relationships in bibliographic data. Descriptions produced using the instructions of RDA are intended to be compatible with any coding schema, including the data environments used for existing records created under the AACR2 rules.

UNICODE

Unicode is a computing industry standard for the consistent encoding, representation and handling of text expressed in most of the world's writing systems. It supports more that 150 languages to create bibliographical records in multilingual formats. Developed in conjunction with the Universal Character Set Standard and published in book form as The Unicode Standard, the latest version of Unicode contains a repertoire of more than 1,10,000 characters covering 100 scripts and various symbols. The standard consists of a set of code charts for visual reference, an encoding method and set of standard character encodings, a set of reference data computer files, and a number of related items, such as character properties, rules for normalization, decomposition, collation, rendering and bidirectional display order (for the correct display of text containing both right-to-left scripts, such as Arabic and Hebrew, and left-to-right scripts).

Unicode can be implemented by different character encodings. The most commonly used encodings are UTF-8, UTF-16 and the now-obsolete UCS-2. UTF-8 uses one byte for any ASCII character, all of which have the same code values in both UTF-8 and ASCII encoding, and up to four bytes for other characters. UCS-2 uses a 16-bit code unit (two 8-bit bytes) for each character but cannot encode every character in the current Unicode standard. UTF-16 extends UCS-2, using one 16-bit unit for the characters that were representable in UCS-2 and two 16-bit units (4 × 8 bit) to handle each of the additional characters.

Users Services

The cataloguing/OPAC module of ILMS can provide the following services;

Current awareness/ bibliographical services : In principle, 'Current Awareness Service' and 'Bibliographic Service' are the same while CAS is generated periodically; bibliographic service is created 'On Demand'. One can select appropriate options and provide filters if needed and generate the report. The report can also save in different formats (in .pdf format/Excel), print it and also send it by email to the users.

Online Public Access Catalogues

The OPAC has simple and advanced search facility with the minimum information for each item including author, title, corporate body, conference name, subject headings, keywords, class number, series name, accession number or combination of any of two or more information regarding the item. Major functions provided in the OPAC module are:

- Simple Search
- Boolean Search
- Advanced Boolean Search
- Displaying and downloading of records in MS Excel, PDF or MARC XML and
- Search support for the items that are in the acquisition process in the library.

Reports

Most of the ILMS provides basic and advanced level reports, facilities with standard filter options. User can create multiple templates depending on requirement by selecting fields.

Basic Report : One can generate basic report with limited number of fields with standard filters by class number, titles, collection type, language, shelving location, accession number record ID, subject heading, recent titles, location, accession number (ranges), users name. One has to enter appropriate parameters and filters, as well as select the desired template and get the report.

Advance Report : Allows using Boolean operator by selecting requisite MARC fields, and sub fields too. There are good numbers of filters to limit the search based on user needs.

- Generate spine labels/ barcode labels and book cards; and
- Generate lists, statistics of items added or edited by operator over a specified time period.

2.5. SUMMARY

The catalogue module describes the objectives, advantages, features of computerized cataloguing. Basic requirements, processes and basic job in cataloguing, importing and exporting data from different format based on standards are also covered. Module also highlights various master databases, standards, reports and user services. The module helps to acquire knowledge required to understand the use of computers in library activities.

There are a number of software packages which could be used to accomplish these activities. The main objective is to indicate the factors which must be taken into consideration when studying automation of these routines and to examine how some of the software deals with this work.

2.6. REVIEW QUESTIONS

1. List main works of a computerised acquisition subsystem.
2. Discuss the advantages of computerised acquisition subsystem.
3. Define Acquisitions Procedures in Academic Libraries?

3

Serials Control

STRUCTURE

3.0 Objectives

3.1 Introduction

3.2 Purpose of Serials Control System

3.3 Functions of Automated Serials Control

3.4 Administrative Requirements for Automated Serials System

3.4.1 Creation and Maintenance of Master Database

3.4.2 Subscription and Acquisition

3.4.3 Circulation of Periodicals

3.4.4 Article Indexing

3.5 Output of Computerised Serials Control Subsystem

3.5.1 OPAC

3.5.2 Reports and Lists

3.5.3 Information Products

3.6 Advantages of Computerised Serials Control Subsystem

3.7 Summary

3.8 Review Questions

3.0. OBJECTIVE

The objective of this module is to impart knowledge on the following aspects of Serials Control;

- Definition and purpose of automated serial control
- Advantages of computerized serials control subsystem
- Get a thorough insight into the operations involved in automated serials management in a library
- All tasks involved in serials control including selection, subscription, payment, check in, reminder, claiming, binding and article indexing, etc.
- Implications of computer operations in serials control
- Creation and maintenance of master databases
- Electronic journal management system and
- Advantages of computerized serials control system

3.1. INTRODUCTION

Serials management, an important module of integrated library management system (ILMS) and part of library operations, has become increasingly complex over the years. Serials control is considered as one of the most complicated library function that is labour intensive and demands high degree of attention for accuracy and details. Managing the serials is considered as one of the most challenging task by the librarian, because of complexity in procedures at different stages of selection of titles, obtaining approval for new titles, renewals, placing orders, invoice processing, maintaining check-in details, claiming non-receipts of issues of journal, etc. Serial management also has issues such as merger and acquisition of publisher and titles of journals, splitting of titles, renaming and also discontinuation. Moreover, journals vary in formats and in frequency of publication. However journals are increasing appearing in electronic formats.

During early 1960, libraries started with automation of cataloguing, circulation, acquisition and implementation of OPAC. In 1990 the serials automation started but there were doubts whether it was worthwhile to spend the effort and funds required to convert manual system into automated system that might not accommodate all requirements of the serials acquisition and management processing. Finally, Internet made a revolutionary impact on libraries leading to, innovative transformation of automated library operations and services. There is no longer any doubt about advantages of serials automation although serials control systems are mainly designed to support services based on efficiency in acquisition, collection development and public services

Purpose of Serials Control System

Serial control system variably called as serial control (in SOUL 2.0), Serials (in LIBSYS 7) and Serials Management (in NewGenLib) is one of the most important and complex modules of any Integrated Library Management Software (ILMS). The purpose of a good automated serials control system may be summarized as follows:

- To have effective and efficient control over subscription, renewal and cancellation of serials
- To record and maintain current as well as serials holdings data accurately
- To provide accurate information about funds required and committed as subscription to serials
- To provide necessary management information reports, whenever required
- To reduce labour and time consuming work involved in manual serials control systems and
- To have a good control over receipt of individual issues of journals, reminder for non-receipt of journal titles, binding and related activities.

3.3. FUNCTIONS OF AUTOMATED SERIALS CONTROL

Serial control consists of a number of activities and services often performed manually. The basic functions and activities remain the same as in automated environment. Some of the major functions that can be expected of an automated serials system are mentioned below;

Handling New Subscriptions

- Handling renewal of subscriptions
- Cancellation of subscription
- Budget control
- Department/unit-wise budget

Invoice processing

- Invoice for individual issues, or for annual (calendar/non-calendar) subscription or prorate subscription
- Creation and maintenance of master database
- Recording the receipt of journal issues
- Generating receipts/reminder for expected missing issues
- Managing (sending claims for) missing issues
- Sending reminders

Dealing with "special editions", supplements, and indexes

Dealing with name changes of publication, publisher and merged titles

- Splitting of journals
- Binding control
- Accessioning bound volumes
- Barcoding of accession numbers
- Report generation
- Listing titles of the periodicals received (alphabetical and subject wise)

- Providing hyperlink to the URL of e-version of journals
- Editing & updating of records
- Searching by title, publisher, distributor, sorting by date or volume/issue number
- Option for Web-OPAC
- Table of contents and other personalized information services
- Article indexing
- Indexing of journal articles by author, title, and subject keywords.
- Import and export bibliographic data of serials from one format to another
- Union list and union catalogue

3.4. ADMINISTRATIVE REQUIREMENTS FOR AUTOMATED SERIALS SYSTEM

Administrative requirements of serial set-up are essential pre-requisite and security parameter that need to be defined before one can use serials module. These administrative requirements include vendor management, budget, frequency, delivery mode, binding and collection type etc.

3.4.1. Creation and Maintenance of Master Database

Modern ILMSs are based on relational data model. Each module of these packages centers around on a master database. Any number of additions, modifications and deletions are possible in the master database and these changes are automatically reflected in all the sub modules under that module. Serials control module also follows the same architecture, wherein records created in the master database are available to all the sub-modules under serial control. It reduces data entry work and ensures standardization. Generally, master database in serial control includes following master entries:

(a) Title Master : In this file, bibliographical details of new serial titles are entered after the selection and approval process. This file also includes details of all the existing serials on the basis of some standard bibliographic format. Any number of additions and deletions in the title master file is possible through appropriate options.

(b) Country Master : This file contains names of countries and their corresponding codes for entering details of country of publication in sub-modules of serials control, Country code is generally based on ISO-3166 where each country is represented by two unique characters e.g. the code for India is as per ISO-3166 standards.

(c) Language Master : This file contains entries for languages and their three digit codes as per the ISDS manual.

(d) Supplier/Publisher/Binder Master : This master file contains details of all local and foreign subscription agents, publishers of serials and binders along with their corresponding codes. These codes are generally created locally.

(e) Subject Master : This master file holds lists of subject descriptors and is available in various sub-modules for entering subject group(s) of serials. This master also includes class numbers, corresponding to subjects covered.

(f) Frequency Master : Arrival schedule for check-in of serial is generated based on the information provided in publication frequency master. Therefore, it is necessary to codify various types of frequencies of journals subscribed by the library. Automated master frequency database will help to monitor receipt and non receipt of journal issues by sending reminders.

(g) Budget Master : This file enables creation of income and expenditure heads, various subheads and allocation of funds for serials acquisition. The module also allows transferring funds from one expenditure head to another head depending on the expenditures as per requirements. Serials budget includes entries for budget head, sub-head, period, account name and code, dates, opening balance, amount spent, credit note amount, closing balance etc.

(h) Currency Master : This file contains currency description, codes and exchange rates of foreign currencies in terms of Indian Rupees. The conversion is calculated automatically based on data given in this file. Currency conversion rate can be updated on the basis of GOC/ bank rates in the master file and is reflected in invoice process.

(i) Delivery Mode Master : Publishers and vendors arrange supply of serials by different modes of delivery such as air mail, shipment/postal, hand delivery, etc. Mode of delivery can be used to set lead time for expected date of issues of journals, keep the track of their receipt. Reminder can be sent automatically once the lead period is over.

(j) Physical Media Master : Serials are available in different types of media which are defined in master file. These physical media can be selected for creation of bibliographic record. The physical media will help user to navigate required title in different forms of resources. It may be textual document, CD-ROM, magnetic tape, online, DVD-ROM etc. This file includes description and corresponding codes for different physical media.

(k) Binding type Master : Individual parts or issues of journals are bound volume-wise at the end of year or subscription period. Binding of back volumes of journals is a regular work of serials control section of a library. This file contains different modes of binding (e.g. standard, leather binding, cloth and rexin binding etc.) and their corresponding codes.

(l) Report Master : This file includes formats for

every type of letter required for the generation of outputs such as order letter, cancellation of order letter, reminder letter and claim letter formats. The terms and conditions formulated by the library may be included in the order letter format.

3.4.2. Subscription and Acquisition

The module contains an option that incorporates various details about subscription to particular journal. The information required to subscribe a journal is entered through this option. Once these details are entered into the system, list of titles of journals is generated which is then sent to the competent authority for approval.

Serial control system revolves around the tasks of making new subscription, renewal, and cancellation of subscription. In order to handle the acquisition work efficiently the system should maintain in-process file and a vendor file. The in-process file may contain the bibliographic and order data, as well as invoice data, if required. The system should be able to produce automatic subscription and renewal alerts. Acquisitions through gifts and exchanges should also be supported by the system. The system should provide support for generation of orders, cancellation and re-order, if required. Acquisition of serials/periodical in a library is different from book ordering system. In contrast to books, the libraries subscribe to periodicals regularly year after year against advance payment.

This group of activities involves the following basic jobs:

1. Selection of serials for new subscription
2. Renewal or discontinuation of existing journals/ serials
3. Selection of delivery mode
4. Selection of subscription mode
5. Formulation of terms & conditions of supply

6. Selection of vendors
7. Approval from authority
8. Ordering and renewal
9. Payment
10. Receipt of bound volumes
11. Reminder generation
12. Adjustment of advance payment for non-receipt of journal issues
13. Preparation of lists of subscribed journals, new arrivals and serials holdings.

3.4.3. Circulation of Periodicals

As a general principle, journals/periodicals are not issued like books. However, to meet specific and essential requirements in special libraries, bound volumes or loose issues of periodicals may be issued only for short period of time, overnight or for a day. This restriction is necessary to avoid gaps in journal volumes or issues as missing issues or lost issues cannot be replaced easily. So for such short-term issue/return, the ILMS should have the provision of issue/return and the option for "on-premise" issue is also available during the office hours or overnight issue may also be allowed. Otherwise, the librarian must get the software suitably customized to get this facility incorporated in the ILMS.

3.4.4. Article Indexing

Article indexing is done to facilitate article level access to the content that appears in each issue of a serial subscribed by a library. A standard data input format is used for entering details of every article that appears in a given issue of journal. Such format can be the one prescribed for MARC, CCF, etc. Integrated Library Management Softwares (ILMSs) usually have a module or sub module for building article index database. Usually article indexing becomes necessary when externally published indexing and abstracting services do not cover the core journals in a given discipline.

In absence of external indexing services, libraries can consider article indexing using ILMS. The first step of article indexing is to determine the bibliographic format of articles to be entered into the system. The input in format article indexing should include some mandatory data elements that are essential to provide basic details of an article. A library must follow a subject thesaurus for the standardization of keywords or descriptors. A number of computer generated services like current awareness list, subject bibliographies, author bibliographies, recent arrival list etc. can be provided to users on the basis of article indexed in the database.

Check-in : One of the most important features of a serials control system is its check-in capability since it is a highly repetitive operation, it must be fast and friendly to be useful to the library staff. There are two basic methods in which the system can be devised to check-in serials. They are by editing holdings statement and by prompting for expected issues. In the first method, the operator has to input the check-in data into the system such as volume number, issues number and additional information such as accompanied materials or supplements. While, this method is very flexible, it can be inconvenient and time consuming. In the second method, the system can predict the expected issue. If the predicted issue matches with the one in hand which is to be checked-in, with minimum number of keystrokes, the issue can be checked-in.

However, this method is possible only for those serials which have predictable pattern of publication and the expected issue can be predicted based on some frequency cycle. If the checked-in issue is not the one expected but is a later one, the system, should automatically mark the gap. On the other hand, if the checked-in issue is not the expected one but earlier one, the system should be able to find out whether the issue details correspond to missing (gap) or whether it is a duplicate issue. In either case, the system should be able to update suitable file/records with minimum intervention of operation.

A good system supports the check-in of multiple copies of an issue on a single check-in transaction even when these copies are accommodated in separate copy records. In the interest of efficiency, the system should also support check-in of special issues, combined issues, supplements, "come with" issues and so on.

Claims : The most frequently faced problem in serials management is the non-receipt of issues of a journal in time. In manual system, it is difficult and time-consuming process to identify the non-receipt of journals and for sending claim notices for missing issues. With automation, identification and claims for such issues becomes easy and takes much less staffs time to accomplish the task.

The system should automatically identify the issues that should be claimed. Some claims maybe automatic and may cause the system to trigger generation of claim notices without or with minimum staff intervention. Other claims will be semi-automatic, in the sense that they require staff review prior to generation of claim notice. Certain situations demand for forced claim i.e., claiming for an issue through operator initiation. The system should have facility to handle all the three situations mentioned above.

The system should be able to automatically identify and produce claim notices for relevant issues on:

- Failure to receive a new order within a library in a specified period;
- Failure to receive the next issue within the expected time frame;
- Receipt of an issue later than the expected time frame;

- Receipt of fewer number of copies in case the library is subscribing for multiple copies.

The system should generate follow-up claim. The criteria for generating such claims may be one suitable to the individual library's practice. Although the system may support issuance of any number of claims, generally a maximum limit is fixed since the probability of receiving the issue after that limit is low.

Computerized Binding Management : Binding management is particularly important in serials control system. It is a common practice in libraries to bind the completed volumes for archival storage. An automated system should be able to indicate when an item is ready to be sent for binding. It is very helpful feature to assist in work scheduling and to spread the binding workload evenly throughout the year. The system might support a variety of approaches for determining, readiness for binding including:

- Upon full receipt of a specified number of issues;
- Upon receipt of the final issue in a specified level of enumeration hierarchy; and
- At regular intervals as specified by the library.

The system should be able to provide on-demand lists of serials ready for binding. The binding sub-module includes following functions:

Binding set selection : This step involves the work of selecting the relevant issues meant to be sent for binding. The selection follows entering of volume and issue number, binding type, colour and embossing type by using drop down menu.

Order process : In this step the software has to generate order letter giving details of the types of binding, no. of volumes for each type of binding, expected date of delivery, payment, etc.

Receiving : This function includes receiving of

bound volumes as per binding order, checking of the quality of binding and accessioning of bound volumes. It also has provision to enter receipt date, classification number, location, etc. and to send reminders for faults in completing the binding jobs and delivering.

Payment : Payment work starts with invoice processing for binding, generates payment release note or order and finally record all the details of payment (e.g. cheque /DD number, date, amount, budget head, payment acknowledgement receipt number and date, etc.).

Reminder : It is meant for generating reminder letters to be sent to the binders in case of any delay in receiving the bound volumes. Binding sub-module should generate list of overdue items.

E-Journal Management

With the advent of e-journals in the 1990s, the serials management in libraries has created new challenges to the serial managers. Electronic journals are changing rapidly like other resources and such their management has to cope up with these changing practices. Although the basic subscription and renewal management are nearly similar in case of print as well as electronic journals management, there are different sets of management strategies and tasks required for e-journals. Electronic resources collections differ from more traditional print collections due to technology, pricing structure, bundling of journals in various subject collections, negotiation of prices and terms and conditions, contract negotiation, and access issues that are inherent in the resources procurement and maintenance.

These tasks, typically associated with electronic journals, can be grouped in the following six categories associated with the life cycle of electronic journals. The typical e-journals lifecycle, as proposed by Oliver Pesch involves the following steps:

- Acquisition of e-journals
- Accessibility of e-journals
- Administration
- Support
- Evaluation
- Renewal

3.5. OUTPUT OF COMPUTERISED SERIALS CONTROL SUBSYSTEM

Computerised serials control subsystems are designed to manage group of routine clerical chores, and act as MIS tool for the library authority. Such systems are able to answer to various user queries in online mode and also generate information products on demand. As a result outputs of such systems are quite helpful and may be grouped into three basic categories – OPAC, Reports and Off-line information products.

3.5.1. OPAC

Generally, the OPAC module of automation packages provides separate option for online searching of serials database of library. OPAC for serials supports searching by:

- Title
  - Current titles
  - Complete holdings
  - Key title
  - Linked title
  - Variant title
- Subject
  - Broad subject heading
  - Subject divisions, descriptors and class number
- Publisher
- Title history

  - Title split
  - Title merge
  - Title change
  - Title holdings
- ISSN

Free text OPAC supports both simple and composite searching along with the application of Boolean operators (AND, OR, XOR, NOT), positional operators (SAME, WITH, NEAR, ADJ) and relational operators (less than, greater than, equal to, less than or equal to, greater than or equal to, not equal to). OPAC also enables users to specify the amount of bibliographic data to be displayed during retrieval.

3.5.2. Reports and Lists

Several reports, letters and statistics can be generated by the automated serials control system. A representative list of such products is as follows:

- List of suggestions
- List of approved titles
- List of titles order
- Subscription overdue list
- List of titles cancelled
- Order letter
- Payment report
- Title report by
  - Alphabetical order
  - Language
  - Subscription
  - Physical media
  - Budget head
  - Department
  - Class number

- Supplier
- Receipt mode
- Delivery mode
- Location
- Country
- Publisher
- Status
- Frequency

- List of issues received
- List of non-receipted issues
- List of missing issues
- List of issues by status
- Reminder letters
- Binding reports
- Binding details
  - Binder wise
  - Title wise
  - Binding received
- Payment details
- Accession register
- Title history reports by
  - Title changed
  - Title split
  - Title merged
  - Title holdings
- General reports by
  - Publisher
  - Vendor
  - Binder
- Statistical reports
  - Yearly and monthly reports

- Subject wise statement
- User's usage statement

These reports can be consulted online or printouts can be generated in off-line mode.

3.5.3. Information Products

Information products of serials control section of a library are generated in offline mode and form the base of various user services. These products are originated either from article indexing activities or serials catalogue database and produced on demand.

Information products from serials catalogue database:

- List of recent arrival for issues of a group of journals (as selected by users);
- List of journals available on a particular discipline;
- Discipline-wise holding list of serials;
- Title wise holding list of serials;
- Union catalogue;
- List of current subscription;
- List of currently available indexing/abstracting journals; and
- List of serials status.

Information products from article indexing:

- Table of contents service of a group of journals (as per user selection);
- Compilation of subject bibliographies;
- CAS and SDI services in online and offline mode;
- Online database searching and retrieval;
- Altering services on specific topics (online/off-line);
- Compilation of abstract bulletin on any given topic;
- News compilation services; and
- Product compilation services

3.6. ADVANTAGES OF COMPUTERIZED SERIALS CONTROL SUBSYSTEM

Serials management is possibly the most complex process in a library. It involves a lot of time bound routine activities that require accuracy and precision. In special libraries, periodicals are the most important resources and take the lion's share from the library budget. The optimum utilization of these resources demands application of ICT as a management tool.

The advantages of automated serials control subsystem are:

- It improves the speed and accuracy in serials control activities
- It can generate various reports in required formats for MIS activities
- It ensures timely reminders generation and better binding control
- It offers easy creation and maintenance of article indexing database and thereby helps in providing a number of user services on demand in many forms.
- It facilitates online access to the serials database from anywhere, anytime in any format
- It predicts the arrival of journal issues and generates schedules for receiving journal issues
- It helps in the export and import of cataloguing data for serials received by the library
- In an integrated serials control module, the master database supplies most of the bibliographical, financial and administrative data at the time of data entry. This approach ensures standardization of entries and also eliminates data redundancy and
- It supports generation of a variety of information products and user services in the desired form and formats.

3.7. SUMMARY

The module covers objectives of serials control with basic concept and definition. It also highlights importance of administrative requirements for automated serials control for creation of master databases and its functional logical link with other operational modules. More emphases are given to operational ICT application techniques and tools. Also describes the process of automated function of serial control like subscription, payments, check in, reminders, binding process, title history, article indexing, e-journal management and advantages of computerized serials control subsystem. Modules coves generation of various reports related to the sub modules.

3.8. REVIEW QUESTIONS

1. What are the basic functions of a computerised serials control subsystem?
2. Enumerate important information products of computerised serials control subsystem?
3. List out various reports required for serials management?

4

Library Services

STRUCTURE

4.0. OBJECTIVES

- To understand the users and kinds of library services
- To know the overview of library services
- To study Requirements for Library Services in automated environment
- To know digital media archiving
- To study database search services

4.1. INTRODUCTION

The libraries have transformed drastically from storehouses for books and journals to the powerhouses of knowledge and information since the middle of the 20th century. The information and communication technology is responsible for this revolution. The very existences of libraries are dependable on users' satisfaction. Users are getting satisfied when the library is able to rise to his or her expectation or meet the actual needs. A quality service is said to be one, which satisfy the users' expectation resulting a good experience. Throughout the history, libraries were mainly concerned with collection development and processing. The library professionals gave less concern to quality in product and services, never checked whether the users were satisfied or not.

Gradually the social and economic changes have prompted the libraries to develop services. The staff has a vital role in the satisfaction of users. The library being a service organization, its prime objective is to provide the right documents, information and services to its users. Only the users' satisfaction survey will facilitate the assessment of their satisfaction with products and service offered.

There are various methods, tools and techniques to measure, control and improve the quality of library services. Quality measurement and evaluation assumes great importance in modern libraries, as it brings immense benefits to the library as well as user community.

We are utilising ICT as a tool (such as Library Management Software (LMS), Library Services Internet, Telecommunication etc.) to serve our users right information at the right time, and the father of reference and information services, suggested in 1876 four basic functions in the area of library services–

Instructing the User : It is intended to help users to learn how a library is organised so that they could take advantage of knowledge contained in information resources.

Assisting the user with his/her queries : It is intended to provide reference and information services that involve either finding the required information on behalf of the users, or assisting the users in finding information.

- Aiding the users in selection of good works: It is the link between librarian's knowledge of the collections and needs of the users. It is intended to guide users in selecting the most appropriate information sources and services.
- Promoting the library within the community: It is intended to relate the activities of the library to the needs of its parent community. It helps to make the library visible in the community. The success of any library depends on the recognition by the parent community.

4.2. OVERVIEW OF LIBRARY SERVICES

The primary objective of a library, irrespective of type or size, is to promote the use of its resources. Library services bring together the document or information sources and their users by personal efforts of the library staff. User's information requirement depends upon the purpose for which he/she is seeking information. Library services satisfy information need of users through dissemination of information resources. The information dissemination activities may be accomplished in two ways

– on the basis of expressed demands or in anticipation. In this section we will study different facets of library services.

4.2.1. Information Sources, Resources and Services

A document gives information or facts. Documents are records of human observations and thoughts, available in many forms and formats. A document in any form can be a source of information. Information sources have two components: conduit (the physical facilities used for gathering, storing, processing and distributing information) and content (the information sources and elements). Information sources become information resources when these are organised and institutionalised in some way, and can thus be reused.

Libraries perform the following activities for optimum use of information sources (Levitan, 1982):

- Develop access mechanism to information sources;
- Provide seamless access to resources;
- Manage and maintain resources;
- Design, develop and disseminate information products and services; and
- Repackage and distribute its products and services;

Information sources can be categorised on the basis of their physical forms, information contents, nature of presentation etc. Denis Grogan divided information sources into three groups (primary, secondary and tertiary sources) on the basis of their information contents. A library should organise information sources to provide services to users. Library services may be provided in anticipation or rendered in response to specific query/ request. Library services should be designed and disseminated keeping in view the information need of users.

4.2.2. Users of Library Services

Libraries are social institutions. Almost all the major human activities like education and training, research and development, industry and business, government administration etc. require active library support. Users of library include students, teachers, researchers, planners, doctors, lawyers, businessmen and people from different walks of the society. Information need of users may vary widely. However, Melvin Voigt showed that there are four types of information requirements or approaches. These are:

1. Current approach, in which users require current information to keep themselves abreast of the nascent developments in the field of their specialization/ interest.
2. Everyday approach, in which users seek some specific piece of information, say, in the form of facts required in the day to day investigation.
3. Exhaustive approach, in which information is sought when a user/ researcher wants to have a comprehensive detailed information about a specific topic on the field of study.
4. Catching up or brushing up approach, in which a user requires information pertaining to related subject fields to catch up with the latest developments in the subject in which he/ she is not an expert.

4.2.3. Type of Library Services

Libraries provide a variety of library and information services to satisfy different information requirements of users. Here the researcher mentions library and Information services are as under.

1. Reference Service : Reference services help users to locate and obtain specific pieces of information from information sources such as reference books, catalogues, directories, files, abstracting and indexing periodicals, databases (online and CD-ROM) and other reference materials. Library personnel may either help users in searching (direct search) or they themselves do the search for users (delegated search) in online or offline mode. Reference service is subjective because of its stress on personalized service. Instruction has objective connotations about it because it encourages the user to independent study. About the Rangnathan reference service was the essence of librarianship.

2. Referral Service : Referral services aim to refer users to the sources of information such as secondary publications, information units, professional organizations, research institutions and specialists/ experts. Such services do not provide the documents or information required by the user for his/her query but give the direction where available. Librarians utilize directories and databases on sources, specially designed and developed for rendering referral services.

3. Current Awareness Service (CAS) : CAS satisfies users' current approach to information and thereby keeps them up-to-date in the field of their work. The important characteristics of CAS are as under:

(i) It is a technique of communicating current information to users.

(ii) It provides latest developments in a subject field and does not provide answer to any specific query.

(iii) Generally covers a broad subject area and supplements the user's own channel/media of obtaining information.

(iv) It is known for the speed and timeliness.

(v) It is meant for use before its contents are absorbed by secondary publications like abstracting and indexing journals.

CAS may be provided through variety of media and channels such as current awareness lists, current contents, routing of periodicals, list of research in progress and forthcoming meetings/seminars/conferences, newspaper clippings etc.

4. Selective Dissemination of Information (SDI) Service : SDI is a special type of current awareness service. It provides each user with the references of documents to their predefined areas of interest, selected from document published recently or received during a particular span of time. In 1950s, H. P. Luhn first coined the concept of SDI as a computer mediated information services. The workflow of SDI service is based on the following steps:

(i) Create users' profile.

(ii) Create document profile.

(iii) Matching the User's profile and document profile.

(iv) Give the notification to users.

(v) Take a feedback from the users.

5. Literature Search Service : It is an extension of reference service. This service includes the following steps:

(i) Analysis of the search parameters of a query.

(ii) Formulation of a suitable strategy for searching different information sources.

(iii) Identification and choosing of most appropriate sources to be searched and the order of searching them.

(iv) Understanding of retrieval features of online databases and CD-ROM.

6. Document Delivery Service (DDS) : Document delivery is a key element in access to information. Unless the documents required by the user are available to him/her, all the other services are of no use. DDS is a complex process and is concerned with supply of documents to users on demand in required format. DDS is the last point in this chain of information services that actually locate the required document and supplies it to users in required format. Electronic DDS supports delivery of documents in digitized form at anytime from anywhere.

7. Translation Service : In the area of science and technology about half of the world's literature is published in languages other than English. Access to non-English literature by people who know English is possible through translations. Translation services thus help in the global access of information. In India, DESIDOC, NISCAIR, IASLIC, ONGC, BARC, BHEL, DRDO laboratories and several wings of the Ministry of Defense and Ministry of Science and technology provides translation facilities.

8. Web-OPAC Service : Web-OPACs are next generation of OPACs. Web-enabled OPACs allow users to search library catalogues and access other services from any client at Library Services anywhere at any time. It allows users to search for the bibliographic records contained within a library's collections. It helps to users for find out necessary information and removes the time barriers. The users access the Web OPAC service with a standard web browser connect as a client machine because the mechanism does not require installation of any additional client-side software.

9. Article Indexing Service : Modern automation packages also provide facility to create and index database of articles or papers published in the journals subscribed by the library. The abstracts of papers/articles may also be included in the database. Such a database allows specific and combined searching by author, title, keywords etc. and produces number of user specific services like table of contents services, compilation of subject bibliographies and generation of CAS, SDI, etc. in online and off-line mode.

10. Lending Service : Lending service provides facility to allow books and other library materials to be read elsewhere by users. This service increases the use of library collection. Computerized lending includes following value-added user services

(i) Quick issue, return and renewal of books and other library materials.

(ii) Automatic display of document availability and possible date of availability, display or printing of documents borrowed by a member.

(iii) Quick generation of fine receipts;

(iv) Issue of member ID card with photograph;

(v) Membership history in the form of list of documents issued and returned by a member during his/her membership tenure.

(vi) E-mail reminders for overdue books.

(vii) Reservation of document by users through OPAC/ Web-OPAC, if it is on loan.

(viii) Inter library loan (ILL) services for documents not available in the local library.

RFID and smart card based circulation system allows self-issue and self-return of documents, secure use of library resources and personalized access to public domain resources.

11. Union Catalogue and ILL Service : Union catalogue is a collection of bibliographical details of resources belongs to a group of libraries. No library of the world can purchased all resources. Union catalogue helps user of one library to check the availability of required documents in other libraries, if not available in the stock of local library. Union catalogue is the result of co operative processing works of member libraries of a resource sharing network or consortium. These are available in the form of CD-ROM databases or online databases. Rowell initiated U.C. Berkeley's first program of inter library lending in 1894, with the California State Library as partner. Inter library loan (ILL) service handles the processing related with the borrowing of items from collections beyond that of the local library. ILL service acts as a central service in resource sharing activities.

12. Electronic Document Delivery Service : Document delivery has always been at the heart of services offered by libraries. Due to the digitization of document; it is possible to make more efficient through the introduction of electronic document delivery. The document delivery service is an integration of document discovery, the location of a supplier, request and delivery. It takes many forms, deals with variety of formats and involves a number of intermediaries. The different types of documents delivery services as under.

(i) Library networks and consortia based services.

(ii) CD-ROM based services.

(iii) Suppler and agent base services.

13. Outreach Services : Outreach services aim to automate the processes required to deliver materials to the home-bound and other patrons who cannot physically enter the library. Automated library systems also offer community information services in the form of list of names and addresses of local organizations or persons, local leisure facilities, employment etc. Outreach services allow creation of user interest profiles, reading histories, easy selection, delivery and return of items. Access to outreach services and community information service is often integrated with OPAC.

14. ICT Base Library Services : Information Communication Technology (ICT) has made significant impact on all spheres of human life. For the Libraries, ICT's has tremendously changed the Management of Resources or House Keeping Operations as well as the way services are delivered. IT application tools and Integrated Library Management Systems are largely used in housekeeping operations, like acquisition, cataloguing, circulation control, serials control etc. In the library, Internet has been used extensively as a resource as well as a tool to deliver the Library and Information Services. Library provides the following ICT base service to their users.

(a) Full text Database services.

(b) CD-ROM Database Services.

(c) Web-based information services.

15. Reprography Services : Reprography means reproduction of documents by photography or xerography, Reprography service is useful for information dissemination. This service provides with charges. Today, reprography plays a very important role in the transmission of knowledge in the library resources and services. Introducing Reprographic services helped to preserve the document from stealing or mishandling.

4.2.4. Requirements for Library Services

A library must develop information services appropriate to its community. These services should take into account information seeking behaviours, information needs, and service expectations of members of the community. The requirements for design, development and dissemination of library services are:

Resources : Libraries should develop comprehensive information resource collection and formulate collection development policy consistent with the goals of its institution or community.

Access : Libraries should support state of the-art computing and communication methods for accessing information resources by its users.

Personnel : Information services staff should endeavour to communicate effectively with the full range of library's clientele and must have knowledge and preparation appropriate to meet information needs of users.

Planning and Policy : The scope of library services should be based on realistic planning and applicable policies and procedures.

Interface : The user interfaces for online services must support easy navigation and provide links to internal and external online resources.

Evaluation : The library should regularly evaluate its information services to ensure that the services help to achieve institutional goals and those goals reflect the needs and interests of the community served.

4.3. LIBRARY SERVICES IN AUTOMATED ENVIRONMENT

Libraries are always at the forefront of the latest technologies to find new ways to optimize the management of libraries and resources, and to provide improved services. Automated library systems, apart from supporting housekeeping operations and management of information services also act as document management systems. It stores documents in digital form and provide appropriate retrieval mechanisms so that individual documents, or sets of documents can be retrieved against specific query or on any given topic. In some systems, the document may be held in print form or microfiche and only the index is in electronic form. Automated system also monitors the whereabouts of documents so that library staff and customers can be aware of the availability and status of the documents in collection. The range of services offered by automated library systems can be placed into three broad groups – user services, MIS support services and digital media archiving.

4.3.1. User Services

These are designed with a focus on the services to customers and offering real benefits to them. These are:

OPAC Service : It is a fully integrated system with other module, acceptable through LAN and WAN. It allows users to

1. make combined and specific search for all formats, i.e. books, journals, computer files, maps, sound recording, musical scores, visual materials,

manuscripts and archival material).

2. To find a level of records.
3. To see standard and customized display of records.
4. To know item level circulation status information in real time
5. To search multiple words and phrases
6. To apply various search operations
7. To indicate the field to be displayed for retrieval.

OPAC is mirror of library collection. Its objectives are

1. To locate resources in a file or database
2. To identify resources
3. To select specific item appropriate to the users need
4. To acquire or obtain access to an item described
5. To navigate a bibliographic database.

Web OPAC service : Web-OPAC is next generation of OPAC. It allows users to search library catalogues and access other services from any client at anywhere at any time. It solves the problem of space and time barriers in libraries and their services rendered. A web-browse standard machine can act as client server.

4.3.2. Article Index service

There are many libraries having modern automation package provide facilities to create a database of articles published in journals subscribed in the library. Such databases are helpful to patrons to search the information by author, title, and keywords etc. It also provide table content services, compilation of bibliographies, and providing CAS and SDI services offline or online.

4.3.3. Lending services

Library provides lending facilities to the patrons to read or consult the material elsewhere. It increases the use of library collection. Automated lending service give value added services as under-

(a) Speedy circulation of material,
(b) Display of documents available or newly arrived in library,
(c) Quick service to generate fine receipt.
(d) Issue of member ID with photographs.
(e) E-mail reminders,
(f) Reservation of documents,
(g) CAS service,
(h) SDI service,

4.3.4. User Support Service

There are variety of users utilize the library for their information need. No library is independent and hence it has to be depended on other libraries and their resources. Union catalogue or a database of more than one library helps the patrons via resource sharing network or consortium. These are available in CD-ROM databases or online databases. ILL services also help.

User support service provides guidance to users as how to make most effective and efficient use of computerized library. The following are user support service:

1. User orientation programmer,
2. Multimedia presentation,
3. Customization online tutorial,

4.3.5. MIS Support Service

There are library management software's contains huge data related to document, staff and user. This database after its extraction, summarized and analysis help in accessing information about management activities like planning, decision making, and reports of items, order, status, overdue vendors, exchange rate and price change, items issued, return and reserved and visited members.

4.3.6. Digital media archiving

The digital archiving system facilitates the users to access information about text, image audio-video clips of material collection, with the help of web browsing. The services provided are-

(a) Full text and metadata based documents with library textural information,

(b) Linking full text digitized documents with library catalogue.

(c) Offering personal information environment to users for accessing information through customized interface,

(d) Providing single layer interface for locally digitalized material like CD-ROM.

Library services in general and reference and information services in particular refer to the personal assistance provided to users in pursuit of information. The reference and information services, provided to library users may be categorised into three broad groups:

- Information services that involve either finding the required information on behalf of the users, or assisting users in finding information;
- Instruction in the use of library resources and services; and
- User guidance, in which users are guided in selecting the most appropriate information sources and services (obviously user enquiry can range from the simple fact finding type to complex questions requiring consultation and analysis of numerous information sources). The increasing availability of electronic information sources, emergence of web based digital libraries and use of desktop based search tools and agents have changed the notion of traditional reference and information services. The whole array of ICT enabled library services are discussed in the following sections.

4.4. ICT ENABLED LIBRARY SERVICES

Library services in general and reference and information services in particular refer to the personal assistance provided to users in pursuit of information. The reference and information services, provided to library users may be categorised into three broad groups:

- Information services that involve either finding the required information on behalf of the users, or assisting users in finding information;
- Instruction in the use of library resources and services; and
- User guidance, in which users are guided in selecting the most appropriate information sources and services (obviously user enquiry can range from the simple fact finding type to complex questions requiring consultation and analysis of numerous information sources).

The increasing availability of electronic information sources, emergence of web based digital libraries and use of desktop based search tools and agents have changed the notion of traditional reference and information services. The whole array of ICT enabled library services are discussed in the following sections.

4.4.1. Database Search Services

Libraries all over the world are finding vital information through online information retrieval services that provide access to thousands of databases containing both bibliographic and primary source information. Databases are also available as discrete datasets on optical discs like CD-ROM, DVD-ROM, etc. Users can either search these databases directly or through intermediaries (such as library professionals). Databases that are available in libraries for remote access via online search or for local access via CD-ROM/ DVD-ROM can be categorised as:

Reference databases : They refer users to another source such as a document, an organisation, an individual or full text of a document. These may be grouped as:

- *Bibliographic databases* : Provide information on contents, location and summarisation through citations, bibliographic references and abstracts.
- *Catalogue databases* : Provide information on the stock of a given library or group of libraries. These databases generally include monographs, journal titles and other library materials.
- *Referral databases* : Include directory type data such as the names and address of organisations or individuals.

Source databases : Contain original source data and act as one type of electronic document. These are grouped as:

- *Numeric databases* : Contain numerical data e.g. statistics and survey data.
- *Full text databases* : Contain databases of newspaper items, journal articles, patents etc.
- *Alphanumeric databases* : Contain textual as well as numeric data e.g. annual reports, handbooks etc.
- *Multimedia databases* : Contain information stored in a mixture of formats (e.g. text, sound, video, picture animation etc.). All the above mentioned databases are accessible remotely through online services or locally through CD-ROM databases. The search framework of online and CD-ROM databases is quite similar and includes following components:

Formulation : It involves several decisions regarding sources, fields, what to search for, and the search variants. Users need to select first the database(s) to be searched. A search may be conducted against one or more selected fields in a database but a search on specific fields produces precise search result than one on a complete record. The next task is to write actual search statement. In search statement search terms may be represented in various ways (singular/plural forms, synonymous forms, variant spelling etc.) and combined by using various search operators (Boolean operators, positional operators, relational operators, etc.).

The general search techniques are:

Boolean search: It combines search terms according to Boolean logic and allows three types of search AND, OR, and NOT.

Truncation : It enables a search to be conducted for all the different forms of a word having the same common root. The search term may be represented through right-hand truncation or left-hand truncation. For example, the right truncated term catalog will retrieve records containing catalogue, catalogues, cataloguing, catalog and so on.

Proximity search : It allows users to specify the distance (in terms of character) between two search terms in the retrieved result sets. In some retrieval system it is represented as NEAR operator.

Field-level search : It restricts a search to a specific field with a view to obtain more precise results.

Limiting search : It limits a given search by using certain criteria, such as language, year of publication, type of information sources and so on.

Action : In the second step, a search button needs to be pressed to conduct a search and the user is expected to wait till the search process ends.

Review of result : In this step, user views the retrieved results by selecting various display options such as size of display, display format, order of items (by author, title, date, etc.) and so on.

Refinement : If user is not satisfied with the search result, he/she needs to reformulate the search statement and conduct a new search.

Online Database Service During the past 10 to 15 years, several related data processing and telecommunication technologies have evolved and merged to make fast, reliable and low cost online information services a reality.

The components of any online database service include:

- Powerful time-sharing computers
- Interactive retrieval programs
- Telecommunication support
- Access privilege
- Machine-readable databases
- Fast, low cost terminals
- Fast access disc storage devices
- Networks

General Services Web includes a vast array of information resources, including but not limited to:

Listserv and Discussion Groups : Includes a wide variety of topics and provides opportunity to exchange current information and conduct a dialogue;

Community Information : These are local data related to weather, demography, tourist places, historical places, local events, transport etc.;

Government Information : Central, state and local self-governments are providing variety of information on web;

Library Catalogues : Libraries are making their catalogues available over the Internet from all over the world;

Commercial Resources : Financial and commercial data are available from stock exchanges, brokers and other firms;

Bulletin Board : These are electronic newsletters that provide news and factual information;

Patent Information : Almost all the countries are making list of approved patents available through web site;

Electronic Journals : Many primary and secondary journals (indexing and abstracting journals) are accessible through web. Some of these ejournals allow free full-text access. Directories of e-journals on various subjects are also available on the web such as PubList (http:// publist.com/ search.html) and BUBL (http:// bubl.ac.uk/ journal);

Electronic Books and Book Reviews : Electronic books appeared first in CD-ROMs (such as reference books) and now these are available through web. Many electronic books are produced that can be used only with specific readers such as RCA e-Book reader, Adobe e-Book reader, Gemstar e-Books reader etc. Some of the significant e-book providers are net Library of OCLC (http:/ /www.netlibrary.com), Questia (http:// questia.com) and ebrary (*http://www.ebrary.com*);

Theses and Dissertations : Theses and dissertations were unpublished sources of information until recently. These primary information sources are now available in the web sites of universities for consultation and downloading; and

Education and Training Materials : Course materials, interactive tutorials and multimedia presentations ranging from school grade to postgraduate grade are available in web for online and offline learning.

Web is a treasure of information. These information resources are either accessible directly through URL (Uniform Resource Locator) or by resource discovery through web searching tools. The web searching tools are categorised into three groups – subject directory, search engine and meta search engine. Libraries generally offer directory-based access to evaluated and useful information resources and web searching tools. These directories are often integrated with OPAC to provide single access interface to users.

4.4.2. Subject-specific Services

Subject-specific information resources are mainly available in the web through three channels – Academic subject directories, Subject gateways and Digital libraries.

Academic Subject Directories: Web directories organize digital information sources by using metadata schemes, bibliographic classification schemes or subject indexing tools. Digital Libraries: These include e-print archives, subject specific digital libraries and web sites related to theses and dissertations.

4.5. TRENDS AND FUTURE OF LIBRARY SERVICES

ICT has created great opportunities for the future of library services. But we should remember that technology does not determine change – humans do. Library professionals should be able to influence the shape of reference and information services. Library service providers have already incorporated a host of new tools, such as computer, modem, CD-ROM, telecommunication and the Internet, to help their patrons. Library services should aim to serve the community wherever it is located, whether in the library, at home, at work, or traveling around the globe because ICT expands the reach of the library to the community and the community's demands upon the library. As a result, libraries are changing from internally focused institutions to externally focused institutions by the application of ICT in designing library services. Three fundamental features will characterize the library services in future. These are:

Service to the community : Serving the needs of the community is the sole reason for existence of libraries, and will be the sole measure of success;

Four basic functions : Library services will be the products of four basic operations– instruction, assisting with research, recommending sources and promoting the library in the community; and

Personal Service : Personal service is that differentiates the library from other information providers. Therefore, librarians will continue to provide personalised service to patrons. The forthcoming changes in various facets of library services may be predicted in terms of the following features:

Diverse community : Today's communities are much more diverse ethnically, linguistically and economically than those of a century ago. Libraries will have to provide information resources and reference services to people of much wider cultural range than they do today.

Increasing demand for instructional services : Future libraries will be complex information systems. Libraries will offer more information sources in different formats and more access points in an integrated but multi-nodal computing environment. In addition, Internet will provide direct access to an overwhelming amount of information. Under such circumstances, the demand for instructional services-as how to find and how to evaluate information sources will increase.

Decreasing demand for factual information : Internet provides direct access to basic information on almost every topic. Patrons who use Internet can easily find simple facts without intervention by the librarian. This is reflected in the downward trend of reference statistics throughout the world. In future, librarians will receive complex and open-ended research questions that will require librarian's research skills. Development of new tools: While the basic functions of the librarian will remain the same, the tools with which those functions are performed will change considerably. Products such as

Reference 24/7 and LSSI's Virtual Reference Desk is beginning to make remote reference and information services as good as traditional in-person reference service. Technology will continue to provide us with new tools that make our services better and faster.

New role of librarians : Librarians will perform the role of information generators rather than merely information conservators in future. Libraries are going to play a greater part in the publishing process. Projects, such as SPARC (Scholarly Publishing and Academic Resources Coalition), Infomine, Librarian's Index to the Internet etc. are all attempts by librarians to take greater control of information production and/or dissemination. In future, libraries will be selecting, organising, servicing and creating information.

Virtual reference services : It is the reference service initiated electronically, often in real time, where patrons employ computers and other Internet technologies to communicate with reference staff, without being physically present. Virtual reference service includes various communication processes such as chat, video conferencing, Voice over IP (VoIP), co-browsing, e-mail and instant messaging.

Quality services : Future library services will be designed in accordance with the principles of total quality management (TQM). Implementing TQM practices will enable libraries to obtain systematic feedback from users, and will ensure continuous improvement.

In short, we can say that marketing and programme evaluation skills including thorough knowledge of quality management principles and practices will be as important as mastering the technology in our endeavour to retain human mediated assistance to users as an important library service.

4.6. SUMMARY

Libraries are service institutions. They provide information services to the users. The use of ICT in designing and delivery of library services achieves economy, ease, extension (or expansion) and efficiency. ICT helps to provide traditional library services more efficiently to innovate new facilities and capabilities in library services to transform the nature of library services. Library Management Software (LMS) can be utilised to support all the conventional user services like catalogue search, lending services, SDI and CAS services, interlibrary loan services and outreach services. Moreover, LMSs offer web based access, MIS support and personal information environment (PIE). ICT enabled library services help to find out any required information at anytime from anywhere by any one through integrated and networked resources and services.

4.7. REVIEW QUESTIONS

1. What are the advantages of digital media archiving?
2. Discuss the use of Internet in library services?
3. Define any two types of User Services?

Part-2:
Media Resources

5

Media Resources for Libraries and their Preservation

STRUCTURE

5.0. OBJECTIVES

- To understand the Media resources available in libraries
- To know digisation of media resources
- To familiarises the preservation methods

5.1. INTRODUCTION

Major advances and tremendous leap towards progress in the field of computer technology, mass media and communication has provided opportunities for the application and use of these technologies for information management purposes. The fast growth of the Internet and its accompanying business through the use and application of Information Communication Technologies (ICT) is due to the rapid advancement and changes that have taken place in access to technology, processing power, storage capacity, and bandwidth. The dynamic changes in information technology affect information infrastructures at all levels. Nowadays, sources of information are increasingly made available only in the electronic form.

The whole world has become one global village due to the convergence of these technologies. It has made possible information access and retrieval of the information much faster in present times. This communication deals with the various aspects of collection, organization and management of Media Resources.

5.2. MEDIA RESOURCES

Media library can be described as a library having collection of audio, video and multimedia resources. Initially these media resources were typically available on tapes, films, spools, etc. but with IT revolution, resources are available on digital media such as CD's, DVD's and video servers.

5.2.1. Types of storage for media resources

These resources can be stored on various audio, video media like audio cassettes, spools tapes,16mm/ 35mmfilms, VHS, U-matic tapes, beta tapes, ultra tapes, etc. and also on digital media such as CD's, DVD's, etc. The tapes, CD's and DVD's can be of different durations. Present day storage of media resources is on archival servers.

5.2.2. Preservation and archiving of media resources

The master tapes are to be preserved in a dust free and air conditioned environment. The temperature of about 15-22°C should be maintained. The relative humidity factor should be around 40 - 60% RH. The tapes should be kept suitably wound and store the encased tapes vertically upright when not in use. Fasten open-reel tape ends securely before storing. Fix appropriate labels to provided areas. Rewind or forward tapes periodically.

Keep tapes away from stray magnetic fields. The tapes are to be stored in dry environment. It is advisable to follow the above mentioned for long term storage of recorded tapes. Nowadays there are archival servers to store and preserve the media resources.

5.2.3. Management of Media Resources

The collection has to be arranged subject wise or tape number wise. This is for convenience of access and retrieval. Sometimes it is arranged according to the needs and use of the media resources within the organization.

5.2.4. Classification of Media Resources

Once the media resources are organized then the collection has to be classified. For classifying the media resources only the main subject class and secondary class numbers are applied. The library can use the classification schemes adopted by the respective library. Classifying of the contents elevates and enhances their value greatly and helps in subject searches.

5.3. CATALOGUING OF MEDIA RESOURCES

For cataloguing of media resources, title of the program, subject, duration, producer, tape number, year of production and brief synopses of the programme are some of the minimum fields which are given. The same inputs are used for creation of bibliographical data in the database.

5.3.1. Creation of Database for Media Resources

An Online Public Access Catalog system (OPAC) has to be designed for storage and retrieval of data on audiovisual materials and the OPAC is the basic electronic access point to audio-visual materials to find out what is available with the library. The database is classified subject wise by using the Dewey Decimal Classification scheme used internationally the world over for classifying the "Universe of Knowledge".

Keywords, free terms and controlled and faceted vocabulary are used in accessing and retrieving information from the database. The main subjects and secondary subjects help in cross references. "See and see also" terms are used for references and also for linking and retrieving the information using Boolean operators for searches. These methodologies help the search engines and the browsers used in the software to retrieve the data.

The user can access the Video OPAC for getting information on the multimedia resources through one's website. One can use descriptors for retrieving the data by title, master tape number, subjects, synopsis etc. The catalogue can be seen on the Web OPAC by clicking at the library button then going to the library search.

5.3.2. Metadata for Media Resources

The common belief about metadata is that it is just for adding keywords is not true. The metadata gains greater importance because of the development of content management software for managing and accessing the content. These days people are using the terms meta data and meta tags for organizing and managing the information.

There are four broad categories of metadata. Structured metadata describes the information architecture of the document. The metadata elements in this case for video programmers include title, duration, tape number, year of production, synopses, production centre, images etc.

Content metadata identifies documents that are relevant to the subject information. Descriptive metadata helps in identifying the type of document like images so the search is possible and is limited to web content, streaming video etc. Administrative metadata relates to the administrative aspects of the document like the person and department owning the document, relevancy of the document etc.

The documents have to be tagged and stored properly in the database so that the search engines can understand the contents better and provide accurate searches with precision. Metadata can be used to encode information. Metadata helps in sharing of information and knowledge resources that could be accessed by users.

5.3.3. Digitization of Media Resources

Video streaming and audio compression software are already inbuilt in the server software on the Windows environment. The database is designed as per user needs and requirements and as library has a wealth of information resources. Streaming media refers to the synchronized delivery of audio and video content on the Internet.

With the advances in streaming digital technologies, Internet, bandwidth speeds, reliability and development in digital audio and video encoding, it is possible to open the resources locked within the audio video files and make it accessible via streaming media and give a synchronized delivery of audio and video encoded content on the Internet.

This can be received on to a user's desktop as an uninterrupted real time stream. The distribution for the stream from a given source like video tape is broadcast by server application that acts as an interface for users requesting access to the streamed video and information.

An ideal film/movie database on the Web should be constructed with full interactive multimedia components and capabilities which provide an end user with real time control of time based media in a standalone or networked setting.

5.4. TYPES OF MEDIA RESOURCES

The media resources for libraries can be categorised into four types according to their forms. They are paper, film, magnetic, and plastic. Shown below are the different types of media resources available in libraries.

Media Resources

↓

Paper (Print) | Film | Magnetic | Plastic

5.4.1. Paper (Print)

Though this Unit is basically on non-print media, you need to be familiarized with the printed documents available in traditional libraries and their preservation aspects as well. Paper is still one of the predominant medium for storing and transmitting information the world over. Paper based collections available in traditional libraries include books, periodicals, dictionaries, encyclopedias, glossaries, bibliographies, yearbooks, handbooks, directories, biographies, gazetteers, atlases, maps, brochures, folders, pamphlets, etc.

5.4.2. Care, Handling and Storage

The following points can be considered for the care and maintenance of the paper collections:

- Poor quality paper deteriorates rapidly in sunlight. It can be avoided keeping out of the light.
- Paper surfaces and edges damage easily with handling. Various protective devices such as lamination, edge binding and the like can reduce these problems.
- Printed sheets which are produced by spirit duplication generally fade in light. Copies, which are stored, should be kept out of the direct light to

minimise these problems.

- Dirt and grease from fingers can damage paper collections. It can be cleaned with an ordinary eraser.

5.5. FILM

Films are available in different formats viz. filmstrips, slides, cine films and microforms. Let us discuss in detail, their physical formats, size, memory etc.

5.5.1. Filmstrips

Filmstrips are made up of a series of still pictures placed in sequential order on35 mm filmstrips, which are available in two different formats. The formats are single or half frame, and double or full frame. The still pictures, which are stored in filmstrips, can be viewed only using projector or viewing equipment.

5.5.2. Slides

Slides are small units of transparent material containing an image mounted on a rigid format and designed for use in a slide viewer or projector. A mount made of cardboard or plastic is used to hold the film. Sometimes glass is used to cover and protect the film within the mount.

5.5.3. Cine film

This is the most popular medium to distribute films for public. Cine film means as, "a sequence of images arranged vertically, which gives the appearance of movement when projected on to a screen at the right speed". Various formats of cine film are discussed below.

35 mm with sound track : This format is generally used in public cinemas. There is also a double sized frame that means 70 mm size, which is used for major productions.16 mm with sound track: This is the format, which is used for distributing films to small clubs, schools and businesses. The film can be projected at24 frames per second, a reel of 40 ft. (i.e.120m) lasting about 11 minutes (36 ft. or 11m per minute).

The sound track is usually optical, being a white stripe down the side. In some films the white stripe is replaced by a brown stripe which is the same as a thin piece of sound tape. This carries a magnetic sound track with all the properties of magnetic tape, and it can usually be erased. Optical sound tracks cannot be altered in this way.

16 mm silent : This film has sprocket holes on both sides without white stripe down as in 16 mm film to produce sound. The film should be projected at 18 frames per second, a reel of 400 ft (120m) lasting about 16minutes (i.e. 24 ft. or 7m per minute).8 mm standard and 8 mm super film: Earlier, standard 8mm film was the only type of 8mm film available. Later, the sprocket holes which appear in left edge of the films, were designed for 16mm film and equipment, and it became apparent that 8 mm film actually did not need such large sprocket holes in order to function properly. Hence, super 8 mm film was designed with much smaller sprocket holes, and the extra space resulted in a 50% increase in the size of the picture area.

5.5.4. Microforms

When categorising media, the microforms can truly be considered a hybrid. It is the amalgamation of both the print and non print media in that it makes print information available on a film format.

Microform is a generic term for all media of communication used to store miniaturised text or micro images on film or paper. It cannot be utilised or read without magnification. It can be grouped into two categories: a) Serialised (roll) microforms; and b) Unitised microforms.

5.5.5. Serialised Microforms

Serialised microforms store images sequentially on a continuous roll film. One has to pass through all the images (before it on the roll), to locate an image. This category includes open reels, cartridges, and cassettes.

Open Reel Microfilm : It is a continuous roll of 16mm or 35mm photographic film that wraps around a spool. It is used to store a large amount of miniaturized text and/or micro images which can be magnified and copied only with the aid of a traditional reader/printer or a reader/scanner. It usually comes in 100 foot lengths, though it can come in lengths of up to 215 feet.

Microfilm Cartridge : It is simply a roll microfilm which has been placed in a compact plastic holder that is self – threading in compatible retrieval equipment. It requires special insertion and material equipment. It protects the film from fingerprints and dust.

Cassette : like a cartridge it houses a roll of microfilm but different in that it contains both a feed and take – up reel. The main advantage of a cassette is that the film does not have to be rewound before it is removed from a reader, and the image can be kept in position for later viewing.

5.5.6. Unitised Microforms

Unitised microforms are images that are cut or created in units and placed in special holdings. It is possible to locate each image directly. This type of microforms include microfiche, aperture cards, and jacketed microfilm.

Microfiche : It is a card shaped sheet of photographic film, usually 3 × 5 or 4 ×6 inches in size designed to store miniaturised text and/or micro images that are arranged in standardised columns and rows. Microfiche can be produced from duplicated jacketed microfilm, from source documents using a step –and –

repeat camera, and from Computer Output Microfiche (COM). On a fiche, 98 pages at a reduction ratio of 24x and 270 pages at a reduction ratio of 48x can be fitted. It is possible to read the title without magnification as the top of the microfiche sheet contains identification information like jacketed microfilm.

Aperture Cards : An aperture card is a keypunch card with a rectangular window with either one frame of 30mm or several frames of 16mm microfilm inserted into the window. The microfilm is directly affixed to the card or it may be inserted into a thin jacket which is itself fixed to the card. The size of the card is generally 187 × 82 mm. These cards are mostly used for large engineering drawings.

Jacketed Microfilm : A microfilm jacket is a fiche sized acetate or polyester carrier. It contains 3 to 8 sleeves or channels into which strips or single images of either 16mm or 35mm roll films are inserted. One jacket can hold up to 60images. It can be used for records that are frequently updated. Because a jacket allows a file to be updated, and the new materials can also be inserted into the unused channels.

5.6. MAGNETIC

Magnetic tape is discussed under two main divisions: audio and video in this section.

5.6.1. Audiotape

Audiotape is the most appropriate medium for music recording. Besides music, many types of information like lectures, debates, speeches, poetry readings, book talks, interviews etc. can be expressed through this medium. Tapes are made of plastic and coated with a layer of ferric oxide or chromium oxide. The plastic is either an acetate or polyester. Audiotapes are available in various playing speeds and recording formats (monaural, stereophonic, and quadraphonic) as well as various tracking configurations (2 tracks and 4 tracks).Tapes are commonly available in two formats: open reel and cassette.

Open reel : The open reel was the first format available, and it is gradually being replaced by the cassette and cartridge. Tape reels are available in various sizes, 3, 4, 5 and 7 inches in diameter. Each size can hold twice as much tape.

Cassette : It was first developed by Philips during the 1960s. The standard dimension of audio cassette is 10.2 × 6.4 cm. It can be categorised into two types according to its formats: reel-to-reel cassettes and loop cassettes or cartridges.

The audio cassette tape is approximately 0.39 cm wide. It is reel to reel in design, which permits tape to be advanced or rewound at high speed. There corders and players for cassette run at a standard speed of 4.76 cm per second. The cartridge tape is 0.63cm wide. It being a loop operates only in one direction and at one speed. Cartridge tapes generally run at a speed of 9.52 cm per second.

Both the cassettes and cartridges are simply inserted into the tape recorder, and are ready to be played. Cassettes are labeled with a capital letter C followed by a number, such as C15, C30, C45, C60, C90, C120, which means that cassettes are sold with predetermined playing times. These are C30 (15 minutes each side) C60 (30 minutes each side) C90 (45 minutes each side) and so on.

5.6.2. Digital Audio Tape (DAT)

This is the latest addition to the tape family and it is used in the computer for storing processed data, backing up data stored in disks and interchanging programs and data between organisations.

DAT cassettes are much smaller 7.2 × 5.4 × 1cm (2.8 × 2.1 × 0.4 in), although the tape itself is the same width, 3.8mm (0.15 in). They are available in 60, 90and

120 minutes lengths, although at long-play speed, they can last twice as long, i.e., up to 4 hours. The cassette itself is enclosed, completely covering the tape, and insertion into the machine pushes back a cover and lifts a lid to reveal it. Accidental eraser is prevented by moving a small slider on the back. When the hole is open, no recordings can be made.

5.6.3. Videotape

Videotape is made of chromium dioxide or metal as the major constituent of the magnetic coating. Like all other magnetic tapes, which have been discussed earlier, videotape can also be used to record digital information for computer related equipment.

Videotape is normally available either in open reel or in cassettes like audiotape. Let we discuss in detail the different types of video tapes. Open Reel Videotape: Open reel videotapes are available in ¼, ½, 1 and 2inch widths. 2-inch videotape is used for broadcasting. 1-inch videotape is mostly used for studio production, ½ inch tape is the most popular open reel format for localized viewing and ¼ inch tape is as good as ½ inch videotape. Out of these videotapes, 1 inch is the most widespread one which is used for professional recording and for many broadcast purposes.

Videocassette : Videocassettes containing ½ and ¾ inch videotape are realizing tremendous growth. Now, there are only three systems active in use: U-Matic, which is mainly confined to professional use; VHS, the common system; and8mm video which is used in a number of semi-professional cameras. U-Matic cassette was the first videocassette format designed, and intended primarily for industrial and educational use. It uses 19.05 mm tape at a speed of 9.5 cm per second in containers, 221 × 140 × 32mm. They are available with varying lengths of tape providing recording times of 10, 15, 20, 30, 40, 50 and 60 minutes.

VHS cassette uses 12.65 mm tape at a standard speed of 2.34 cm per second in containers, 188 × 104 × 25 mm. They are available with varying lengths of tape providing recording times of 30, 60, 90, 120, 180 and 240 minutes. VHSC is a much smaller cassette which can be used in cameras to make recording and S-VHS is a new development to improve the quality of the recording and playback.

Cassettes using the small 8mm tape are 9.2 × 6.2 × 1.4 cm. The tape is totally enclosed when not in use, the flaps at the front of the container parting is opened when placed in the equipment. Playback of 8mm cassettes is generally either through a television set attached directly to the camera or through dubbing to a conventional video recorder.

5.6.4. Storage Disks

In this section, let us concentrate on the magnetic disks which are used in the computer as the back-up storage medium for recording information or data and programs. It can be categorized into two kinds: hard disk and floppy disk.

Hard Disk : Mainframe computers use disc packs, but these are stored within the computer service area. More common and increasingly available at relatively inexpensive prices, are hard discs or Winchester discs. These are smooth metal plates coated on both sides with a thin film of magnetic material. A set of such magnetic plates is fixed to a spindle one below the other to make up a disk pack

These are 7.5 to 20 cm (3 to 8 in) discs, kept with the reading heads in sealed, dust free containers, and are usually attached to or part of the computer itself. Storage capacity is up to 300 megabytes of data.

Floppy Disk : Floppy disks are used as secondary storage medium for storing and keeping back-up information or data stored in microcomputers. The floppy disk is made of magnetic oxide coated computer tape material. As the material used is not hard plate but a flexible tape, it is called "floppy disk". It is removable, portable, and widely used medium in libraries. Alteration, such as copying and deleting files or documents, can easily be done in any number of times.

Floppy disks are available in three formats: 8inch; 5.25inch; and 3.5inch. 8inch and 5.25 inch floppies are now obsolete. There is also another form of a disk, about 2inch in diameter, available for recording still photographs shot with special cameras (i.e. digital cameras). About 50 pictures per disk can be stored and the playback is through a television set.

5.7. PLASTIC

Plastic based material can be categorised into three types: transparent plastics; vinyl discs, and optical storage discs. Optical discs are now the most widely used media in IT industry and library.

5.7.1. Transparent Plastic

Overhead transparencies are extensively used in education for lecture, presentation etc. The major types of transparencies are clear acetate (on which information is drawn with a pen), thermal (heat process), and diazo (low speed photographic). The transparencies, which are used with the overhead projector are available in various thicknesses. The thicknesses are commonly ranging from 0.05mm to 0.25mm as either single flat sheets or as rolls.

The rolls are 25.4mm wide and of varying lengths, whereas the flat sheets are usually supplied in three sizes: 26.7 × 26.7cm (10½ × 10½ in.), 26.7 × 20.3 cm (10½ × 8 in.) and 29.7 × 21cm (11¾ × 8¼ or A4). When loose sheets are kept against each other, paper should be inserted between them to reduce the natural adhesion between plastic.

5.7.2. Vinyl Discs

There are two categories of vinyl discs, audio and video, discussed in the following sections:

Audio Disc : Perhaps the prominent audio form is the disc recording. Discs are marketed in various sizes of 17.8cm, 25.4cm, and 30.5cm diameter sizes. The central hole for the spindle is about 7.5mm in diameter. This spindle need not be a tight fit.

Video Disc : The videodisc is similar to an audio disc. The size and shape of the discs are same, and it has grooves. A slight difference is that the audio disc is generally black, whereas a videodisc is metallic and has an aluminized appearance.

A single videodisc contains 108,000 grooves or frames (54000 on each side) and thus has the capability of storing 108,000 pages of printed text or 'still' information. Any particular frame can be retrieved and viewed in less than 3.5seconds, when a disc is used on a player with an electronic accessioning function. Videodisc has already been illustrated in Fig. 6.8 (see two discs appear at last from left in back row).

5.7.3. Optical Storage Systems

Various configurations of optical storage systems are: laser vision, CDs and DVDs.

Laser vision : These discs have been produced in two forms: a continuous moving picture of an hour's duration each side without still picture facility; and a 36 minutes' of duration each side with still picture control (i.e. individual frame/picture is easily identifiable). Two audio channels are also available on each: in the first providing stereo sound; and in the second offering selectable options such as two different languages, or sound effects on one with voice on the other. The discs are usually coloured silver, size, 30 cm (12 in.) in diameter and 3.4 mm thick, and have a centre hole of 35 mm diameter. The disc can hold 54000 individual frames or pictures. In addition, a tele text analogue is also possible, providing the option for other information.

Compact Discs : In 1982, Sony recorded stereo music for the first time on a disc, called 'Compact Disc', transferring analog signals into a digital form. A compact disc is made of polycarbonate with one or more metal layers capable of storing digital information. Compact discs for audio were shown in 1980 and were launched commercially in 1983 by Philips and Sony. The physical size of the disc is generally 12cm in diameter, 1.2mm thickness, and 15mm hole in the centre of the disc. Different versions of the discs, which are available in the market, include CD audio, CD – ROM, CD – V, CD – I, CD – R, CD – RW etc.

DVD (Digital Versatile or Video Disc) : The DVD is the new generation of optical disc storage technology. It has replaced the laser disc, and eventually could replace audio CD and CD –ROM. This disc holds 4.7 GB of data on one of its two sides. It is possible to store a133 minute movie in one side of a DVD. With two layers on each of its two sides, it can hold up to 17 GB of video, audio, still photos or other information, and the access rates of 600 KBps to 1.3 MBps. Comparatively the DVD holds 28 times more data than the CD – ROM disc (see table 6.3). Like CD – ROMs, DVDs are also available in different physical formats such as DVD – ROM, DVD – R, DVD – VIDEO (simply called DVD), DVD – R/RW, DVD + R/RW, DVD – RAM, DVD – VR, DVD – AR, DVD – SR, and DVD – A.

5.8. SUMMARY

In this unit, different types of media resources, print and non – print, have been discussed. Film media, which include filmstrips, slides, cine film, and microforms, have been discussed in detail with figures and illustrations. Magnetic media, which include audiotape, videotape, and magnetic disks, have also been discussed. Plastic media, which include transparent plastics, vinyl discs, and optical discs (CDs, DVDs, etc.), have been explained, with suitable examples. An attempt has also been made to discuss the methods of preservation for handling and storage of all four kinds of media resources separately.

5.9. REVIEW QUESTION

1. List the four major categories of media resources?
2. What are the Print materials available in traditional libraries?
3. Explain type of storage disc?

6

Equipments and their Maintenance

STRUCTURE

6.0. OBJECTIVES

- To know the factors to be considered in maintaining the equipment
- To know their basic features
- To learn about the different kinds of equipment in a library
- To get an insight into the problems with equipment
- To become familiar with the criteria for selecting equipment

6.1. INTRODUCTION

In the previous Unit, you were introduced to different types of media resources based on the varieties of materials viz., paper, film, magnetic, and plastic. Though the paper is a prominent medium, libraries and information centers also procure non - print materials. These are available in different formats viz., filmstrips, slides, microforms, cassettes, tapes, discs, etc. Thus, the materials (except paper collections) need related equipment for their use. The library and information professionals need to acquaint with the non - print materials and the related equipment in order to render effective services to the users. Keeping this in view, we shall focus on different types of equipment with regard to their description, functions, criteria for selection, maintenance etc. in this unit.

6.2. TYPES OF EQUIPMENT

Equipment used for media resources in a library could be categorised in different ways based on the categories of materials such as film, magnetic, and plastic.

Filmstrip Projectors

Filmstrip projection

- A series of still pictures on a 35 mm of film

- Often accompanied by a sound cassette programmed to automatically change filmstrip using a 50 Hz. signal to activate advance
- Almost all programs come with a dual recording; automatic (inaudible 50 Hz. pulse) on one side, manual (audible pulse) on the other.

Formats

- Single frame; most common, held vertically for projection, ½ of full frame
- Double frame; produced on regular 35 mm camera using full frame and held horizontally for projection

Handling filmstrips

- Handle filmstrip by edges to avoid fingerprints
- Filmstrip is inserted upside down and backwards (when you are behind the projector, facing the screen)

Storage

- Best stored in original container
- Cabinets available
- Some projectors use a cartridge

Advantages

- Easily and compactly stored
- Always in proper sequence
- Can project silent strips at own rate

Disadvantages

- Must always be shown in the same sequence
- Easily damaged in handling

Filmstrip Projectors

- Most designed for single-frame filmstrip; but some can handle both and others adapt for slides

- Sound filmstrip projectors use a cassette tape as sound source. Inaudible pulse is used to synchronize.
- A 50 Hz. pulse is usually used, but some have 1000 Hz. Pulseviewer/projector models available

6.3. OPERATING PROCEDURE

1. remove front screen units from case and plug in
2. insert filmstrip upside down as you ace the lens (strip should curl toward screen)
3. hold film along edges and push into slot until it can go no further
4. turn ADVANCE knob until film comes out exit slot
5. turn on projector and turn on lamp (the Dukane has two separate switches, both must be on for advance reverse to work)
6. advance to focus/start frame and focus (frame if necessary)
7. raise or lower base as necessary
8. for sound projection advance filmstrip to frame saying "start the tape here"
9. insert tape, rewind to beginning and push play
10. at end, turn lamp to frame
11. remove filmstrip, rewind by hand
12. when cool turn off, unplug, return to case

Cleaning : Dust off condenser lens with camel's hair brush. Clean front and back of projection lens with lens tissue. Glass pressure plates need to be cleaned or dirt may scratch the filmstrip.

Slide Projectors : Slide Projectors are of different kinds depending on their degree of automation. These are (a) Manual, (b) Semi automatic, and (c) Automatic. In manual projectors, movement of slides behind the lens is done manually causing each to be visible in turn. A lever turns the slides one by one behind the lens in a semi-automatic projector. In Semi-automatic projector the slides are put together in a magazine and not held singly. The system is semi automatic, as the slide cannot be brought back using the lever. It has to be done manually. The management of slides back and forth in automatic projectors is done mechanically. The movement is back or forward depending on the signal. There are two different buttons for forward and backward movement or one button being pressed for different lengths of time for forward and backward movement. There are multi slide projectors also in which two or more machines are attached to it. The action is such that while one slide is being shown, slide in the other machine is being changed and vice versa. Such projectors are controlled using computers.

6.4. CINE PROJECTORS

Cine film consists of a series of still pictures separated from each other by a black band. The projector has a drive and a take up wheel with the lens and lamp in between Cine film with a series of still pictures and a sound track which moves constantly. The pictures are shown separately, the difference being fraction of seconds that gives a view of a continuous film. The separator on the pictures is not visible on the screen as when it is near the lens, the hole is covered making it invisible. The pictures move with jerks, however the sound track moves constantly otherwise it would result in a noise.

6.4.1. Microform Readers

Microforms are available in different formats viz. roll (1.16 mm, 35mm),cartridge, cassette, fiche, aperture card, etc. for which there is variations in thereaders as well. However, the basic principle is the same, i.e., the microform isheld close to the lens so that maximum light passes through the microform formagnification. The evenness of magnification depends on the quality of lens.The closeness of the lens to the microform requires the movement to be donewith caution, otherwise it may go out of focus. There are two viewing systemsviz, front and rear projection. Rear projection system is not preferred as thescreen is unevenly illuminated and excessive brightness causes strain on theeyes. In the front project system, light is bounced off the screen which helps toreduce the bright spot on the screen. To avoid the glare in rear projection,screens are coloured and tinted. Different lenses are provided in microformreaders to allow different magnification as the reduction ratios may varybetween 10x to 48x.

6.4.2. Magnetic Tape Recorders

Message recording on the tape is caused by a change in the magnetic flux around its surface. The signal for the change comes from the recording source which produces electronic translations of the signals. Changing or deleting the message is also caused by the same kind of action. The direction for recording or reproducing/retrieving the signal is sent by different knobs on the equipment. The tape moves from left to right at a uniform speed touching the heads due to a series of spring pressure pads. The area where the message is recorded when touches the head, the message is played. The speed at which the tape moves should be constant otherwise there is disturbance in the visual as well as audio signals. Some cassettes have a Dolby mark on them showing that the recording is Dolby. Such a recording reduces the environmental sounds by compressing the recorded frequencies. A player with a Dolby system provides a better output.

6.4.3. Overhead Projector

It consists of a lamp underneath the film placed on a convex lens. The lightpasses the lamp and the film on to a mirror placed above the film. The mirrorreflects the light from the film to the screen. There is a fan inside that keeps thetemperature under control for the heat generated by the lamp inside the projector.To focus the image of the films, the mirror is changed in position using anadjustable screen.

6.4.4. Record Player

The recording on a disc is in the form of waves in the grooves. The player has stylus which is triangular with a rounded or elliptical tip to read information on the record. The tip of the stylus is made of sapphire or diamond. The stylus moves in the grooves to read information. The weight of the stylus may wear out the record. Thus, the weight of the stylus needs to be optional so that there is no undue pressure on the record.

6.4.5. CD-Player

Recording or reading information on compact discs is done using high powered laser beams. It enables large amount of densely packed data. The laser beam used has no side-effects on health of the user. It moves only when the lid or cover of the CD is closed. The possibility for varied retrieval options makes CD a better sought-after option. The user can access a particular position of the disc and start playing from there. A number of discs can be stacked and accessed in the form of a Juke box. The quality of the output can be controlled through the amplifiers and speakers also.

6.5. CRITERIA FOR SELECTING EQUIPMENT

Maintenance is the key to efficient functioning of equipment. But how often is maintenance required? It depends on the frequency of use. Both, high and low use demand more maintenance. High use causes wear and tear and low use causes jamming of parts, thus there is need for maintenance. Regarding the how of maintenance, there are certain things we all know of maintaining equipment at home also. Besides, the manual that is provided with the equipment is the best guide for the how of maintenance. The do's and don'ts mentioned in the manual should be strictly adhered to. It is also important to note that the librarian should be involved in the basic maintenance chores only and leave the maximum to the expert. The expert is generally the person from the company which has supplied the equipment or its dealer/ distributor/representative or a technician from the organisation of which the library is a unit. It is preferable to have an Annual Maintenance Contract with the supplier for the proper upkeep of equipment.

The following points need to be considered for the maintenance:

Cleanliness : Equipment should be protected from dirt and dust. It should be kept in neat and clean surroundings. When not in use, it should be kept covered. Standard size covers provided by the company that are also harmless to the material of the equipment should only be used. Glasses, lenses and mirrors should be cleaned to remove the grease and dust that passes from users' hands. Care must be taken to use lint free tissues or anti-static brush which is available with opticians. Grease can be removed by breathing on the surface and wiping with a tissue. If this doesn't work, a small amount of spirit may be used but precaution should be taken not to use it near joints otherwise it acts as a solvent. Dirt on glass should not be removed by rubbing or scratching as this would damage it. While cleaning care must be taken not to disturb the position of glass, lens or mirror as it would affect the functioning of the equipment. In case it is not possible to reach the glass, lens or mirror to clean, then use a soft brush (anti-static), particularly if it is linked with a puffer. The work area of the equipment can be cleaned using an anti-static, hard brush.

Oiling : Mechanical parts in equipment need regular oiling to overcome the friction. These days most of the parts are covered in sealed joints, and are lubricated permanently. Still, wherever indicated in the manual that some parts need oiling, it should be done accordingly. The frequency of oiling is also indicated therein. Care should be taken that oil doesn't spill on glass or film surfaces.

Cleaning the Heads : Heads of audio and video players catch dust from the tape. Cleaning of heads can be done by playing blank cassettes available for cleaning. They may be played regularly for the purpose.

Cleaning the Style : The stylus while moving on the grooves of the record picks up dust as well as plastic which need to be removed. The disc can be kept clean using an anti-static brush or cloth. For the stylus, liquids are available which can be used with a brush. The liquid loosens the dirt on the stylus and the brush removes it. Care should be taken not to touch the stylus as this would result in grease accumulating on it.

Cleaning the Headphones, Microphones : Headphones and microphones are used by different people that touch the ears and come close to the mouth which may cause an infection. They may be wiped with cloth soaked in the disinfectant before use.

Cleaning the Optical Storage Discs : Optical Storage Discs are quite sturdy and need little maintenance. But dirt sticking to them may interfere with laser beams. Liquids are available for cleaning, but wiping should be done from centre towards the radius and not in circles as it causes the dust to move from one section to the other.

Cleaning the TV Screens : TV screens attract lot of dust due to the electrostatic attraction. It should be cleaned by cloth soaked in aerosols regularly.

Cleaning Computers : Computers should be kept covered to prevent dust. Keyboards should be cleaned with brush. Liquids should be kept away from it to avoid spilling.

Lamps, Fuses and Plugs Maintenance : Lamps, fuses and plugs are important accessories which may need to be replaced often. It is important that they be replaced according to the specifications as also indicated in the manual. Fuse should be checked regularly for the safety of the equipment. Plugs may develop cracks by careless use and therefore should be replaced in time.

Battery Maintenance : Some equipment runs on batteries. Recommended batteries should be used for the safety of the equipment and should be removed when not in use

6.6. MAINTENANCE OF EQUIPMENT

Librarians have been facing certain problems with equipment that are discussed below:

Availability of Variety of Equipment/Models : The librarian is baffled due to the variety of equipment and their models being available in the market. Different companies offer variety of models causing confusion as well as lack of standardisation. It also causes problem for the user who has to operate them and has to learn the variations.

Obsolescence : Rapid advancements in technology result in regular updating of models thereby user as well as the media material demanding new equipment. The new material is not compatible with the old equipment. If the earlier equipment can be modified and updated to adapt to these materials, it is okay otherwise the librarian has to acquire new equipment. It has been opined that the average life of equipments is 10years if properly maintained and that a librarian should frame plan for 5years when purchasing equipment so as to make effective utilization. Such a policy can be adopted by large and resourceful libraries, but can be a problem for small libraries.

Foreign Equipment : Most of the equipment (especially film based) is not manufactured in India.

Besides being expensive, libraries find problem in their installation and maintenance. Thorough training in usage of this equipment needs to be imparted to the library staff for safety of the equipment and the media resources to be used thereon.

Besides there are some specific problems related to microform readers, which could be enumerated as:

- Different models are needed for different sizes and formats;
- Lack of uniform sharpness on the screen;
- Lack of uniform brightness (hot spot in the middle) on the screen;
- Need to refocus on moving from one page to other;
- Darkened room requirement for equipment use creates problem for normal work to be done in the room;
- Configuration of machines requires users to remain normally in more or less in one position;
- Manufacturer's disinclination to put clear instructions on the machine causing problems to users;
- Image rotation facility not available; and
- Image much less satisfactory than original document.

6.7. SUMMARY

This Unit describes different kinds of equipment based on the varieties of material. It also provides a criteria for selecting equipment which could serve as a guideline while buying equipment. Maintenance is a very important issue for equipment which has been discussed in detail. The Unit also dwells on the problems with equipment and in particular, problems faced by librarians in India while dealing with equipment.

6.8. REVIEW QUESTIONS

1. Mention the different formats of film material and the related equipment?
2. How does a cine projector work?
3. Differentiate between manual, semi-automatic and automatic slide projector?
4. Describe in brief an overhead projector?

Part 3 : Digitization of Media Resources

7

Digitization Concept and Need

STRUCTURE

7.0. OBJECTIVES

- To find methods and technology used in digitization and formation of digital libraries
- The digital library collections has become an attractive and feasible
- To discusses the challenges often encountered during digitization
- To improve preservation of library materials.
- To implications for planning and policy.

7.1. INTRODUCTION

Digital Libraries are being created today for diverse communities and indifferent field's e.g. Education, science, culture, development, health, governance and so on. With the availability of several free digital Library software packages at the recent time, the creation and sharing of information through the digital library collections has become an attractive and feasible proposition for library and information professionals around the world.

Library automation has helped to provide easy access to collections through the use of computerized library catalogue such as On-line Public Access Catalog (OPAC). Digital libraries differ significantly from the traditional libraries because they allow users to gain an on-line access to and work with the electronic versions of full text documents and their associated images. Many digital libraries also provide an access to other multi-media content like audio and video

7.2. DIGITIZATION: DEFINITIONS

The process of converting data to digital format for processing by a computer. In information systems, digitization usually refers to the conversion of printed text or images (photographs, illustrations, maps, etc.) into binary signals using some kind of scanning device that enables the result to be displayed on a computer screen."

also defines digital library as the "library in which a significant proportion of the resources are available in machine-readable format (as opposed to print or micro-form), accessible by means of computers

The word "digital" describes any system based on discontinuous data or events. Computers are digital machines because at their most basic level they can distinguish between just two values, 0 and 1, or off and on. All data that a computer processes must be encoded digitally as a series of zeroes and ones.

The digital libraries store, organize and disseminate digital contents. These contents are created either through digitization of existing printed materials and media documents, or through re-keying/re-composing of existing printed materials and media documents, or through creating new documents in digital formats. The first kind of documents is known as digitized documents, and the later kind of documents is known as born digital documents. In Indian digital libraries both kinds of documents are available. The digitized documents are stored either in image formats or in text formats. If the original documents are available in European languages such as English, French, German and Spanish, the optical character recognition (OCR) software can automatically convert them into searchable digital text format, where qualitative OCR conversion rate is much higher. On the other hand, if the original documents are available in Indian languages such as Sanskrit, Hindi, Bengali, Oriya, Telugu and Tamil, the contents are made available either in image formats or re-keying the texts for the inclusion in the digital libraries. OCR software for Indian languages is still in the developmental or testing stage, where OCR conversion rate is much lower than acceptable rate. The full-text searching is possible in textual documents but this facility is absent in image documents.

7.3. NEED FOR DIGITIZATION

There are three major reasons for digitization endeavours: (i) there is a need to preserve endangered library resources, (ii) improvement of the efficiency of information search mechanisms, and (iii) digitization improves access to library resources. Most libraries are digitizing materials which might be lost in the future, such as old manuscripts, research projects, photo images, analogue maps, non-live musical recordings, government official gazettes and several other historical records. Digitization is useful in preserving precious materials. Making high-quality digital images available electronically will reduce wear and tear of fragile items. However, digital copy should not be seen as a replacement for the original piece, therefore original document should be cared for even after digitization. Preservation remains a secondary benefit of digital projects.

The search mechanisms for information in the traditional library set-up are very slow and inefficient. Libraries in most third world countries are dispersed and uncoordinated. This makes accessing materials in these libraries to necessitate physical contact by users. If these libraries become digitized, such library resources can be assessed online without stress. Online links can be made to existing digital libraries; this will enable users to use materials that are not available in the local library. In fact, it will enable inter-library loan.

Digitization improves access to library resources. By digitizing library collections, information will be accessible to all instead of a group of researchers. Digital projects allow users to search for collections rapidly and comprehensively from anywhere at any time. Digitization makes the invisible to be visible. Several users can access the same material the same time without hindrance. It also removes the problem of distance, as users do not have to travel to libraries that possess the hard copies of library materials before they can access and use such materials. A digital library can be made to serve a region.

7.4. SELECTION OF MATERIAL FOR DIGITIZATION

To begin the process of digitization, first of all, we need to select documents for digitization. The process of selection of material for digitization involves identification, selection and prioritisation of documents that are to be digitised. If an organisation generates contents, strategies may be adopted to capture data that is "born digital". If documents are available in digital form, it can be easily converted into other formats. If the selected material is from the external sources, IPR issues need to be resolved. It is important to obtain permission from the publishers and data suppliers for digitization, if material being digitised is not available in public domain. Moreover, decision may be taken whether to OCR the digitized images. Documents selected for digitization may already be available in digital format. It is always more economical to buy e-media, if available, than their conversion. Moreover, over-sized material, deteriorating collections, bound volumes of journals, manuscripts etc. would require highly specialised equipment and highly skilled manpower.

The documents to be digitized may include text, line art, photographs, colour images, etc. The selection of document, need to be reviewed very carefully considering all the factors of utility, quality, security and cost. Rare and highly required documents and images are given first priority in selection without considering the quality. Factors that may be considered before selecting different media for digitization include:

Audio : The sound quality has to be checked and required corrections made together by the subject expert and computer sound editor.

Video : The video clippings are normally edited on Beta max tapes which can be used for transferring it on digital format. While editing colour tone and resolution is checked and corrected.

Photographs : The selection of photographs is very crucial process. High resolution is required for photographic images and slides. Especially the quality, future need and the copyright aspects have to be checked.

Documents : Documents which are much in demand, too fragile to handle, and rare in availability are reviewed and selected for the process. If the correction of literary value demands much input, then documents are considered for publication rather than digitization.

7.5. STEPS IN THE PROCESS OF DIGITIZATION

The following four steps are involved in the process of digitization. It provides six stages in digitizing documents for a digital library: Registering, Scanning, Optical Character Recognition, Proofreading and formatting and producing the Final Version.

(i) Registering before scanning large number of documents : There is the need to first register them and use a filing system to keep their track. If not, you risk misplacing hardcopies, losing files, skipping steps in the process or duplicating work, perhaps without realizing it. There is also the risk of losing electronic versions of files because they have been misnamed or saved in the wrong subdirectory. Moreover, a good filing system is vital, so everyone in the digitizing team knows what he is supposed to do, and he can fill in for another person in case of absence.

(ii) Scanning documents : It is necessary to clean and dust off the documents to be scanned; make sure that all the pages are present and in the right order. If the document is in poor condition, try to find a fresh copy. If it is a sheet fed scanner, cut the document open to get individual sheets to feed through the scanner. If necessary, you can rebind the documents later. If you do not want to damage the documents, you can photocopy each page and feed in the photocopy through the scanner, though this uses a lot of paper and reduces the quality of the scan. To scan a document on a flatbed scanner, place it face down on the scanner platen or put the pages into the sheet feeder. Then, in the software, choose a setting, resolution and colour and scan each page of the document at the settings you have chosen.

(iii) Optical Character Recognition (OCR) : Optical Character Recognition (OCR) software converts a scanned image into a text file that a word processor can read. To do this, it must first recognize where the text is on the page. The software breaks the text blocks down into lines or into an individual character. It tries to match the image of each letter against patterns it recognizes as an "a", "b" etc. There is a problem to encounter with languages that use Latin scripts with accented characters. As a solution, you should use the OCR software that is specific for language.

(iv) Proofreading : This is the act of making corrections to the document text and layout. This is done in two ways: a. Comparing the scanned text on the screen with the hardcopy and entering the corrections directly into the computer. The word processor's spellchecker will help in spelling errors quickly. b. Printing out the scanned text and comparing it with the original copy. Mark any corrections on the printout, and then enter them into the computer. This is a slower method, but may be the best option if there are no enough computers for each proofreader.

(v) Reformatting : The Optical Character Recognition (OCR) software may produce a document that consists of straight text, no columns, no headers and footers. There is the need to reinsert these by hand or correct where they appear on the page. There may be also need to change the typeface, heading styles and so on, to make the document more attractive and readable. Alternatively, you may be able to adjust the settings of your OCR program to preserve the layout of the page.

(vi) Final Version : For many documents, there is a need to add some information to the text so that readers can identify it easily. As for a book you must make sure that the book title, the author or the editor, the publisher and the publication date are all included. As for chapter in a book, you should include the title and the author of that chapter and the original page numbers in the printed version of the book. As for the journal articles you should include the journal title, the date, the volume and the issue number, the article title and the authors and the page numbers in the original printed journal. In other words there is the need to add Metadata to describe each document.

7.6. DIGITIZATION: INPUT AND OUTPUT OPTIONS

A document can be converted into digital format depending on the objective of digitization, end user, availability of finance, etc. There are four basic approaches that can be adapted to convert from print to digital:

- Scanned as Image Only
- OCR and Retaining Page Layout
- Retaining Page Layout using Acrobat Capture; and
- Re-keying the Data

7.6.1. Scanned as Image Only

A set of scanning instructions is delivered to the scanning workstation operator prior to the start of scanning for every digital conversion project at the Library. These instructions include all document handling procedures, all technical standards, all naming conventions, and all post processing requirements.

The evaluation of technical image quality and adherence to standards generally is approached in two stages. First, scanners are "characterized" through the use of sample images and targets designed to measure tonal reproduction, dynamic range, resolution, noise, color accuracy and additional characteristics that are determined to be of particular importance for a given application. This data helps in the selection of an appropriate scanner for the project and helps operators install, configure, and set the equipment controls properly. Second, a target may be included with every image or on specific occasions such as the first and last image of a document. This data helps insure that the ongoing imaging work maintains the original quality specifications. Historically, the Library has used the USAF 1993 Visual Resolution Test Target (and similar derivatives) to establish that visual resolution is in compliance with requirements. Tonal representation has been evaluated through visual inspection of sample and actual images selected from scanner output.

Now ISO standards for the measurement of the appropriate image quality elements have been approved and the Library has begun to test and characterise scanners through the use of Standard ISO targets as well as with sample images.

The intended to be a listing of proposed requirements for TIFF image header tags required by the Digital Conversion Services (DCS) and applicable to all digitization products for still image content regardless of the original format or method of digitization. The ability to store, access, and preserve content depends upon good metadata, and once finalized, the proposed requirements will serve as the core minimum required tags of metadata for these purposes. To insure DCS metadata requirements are met, images delivered by contractors and internal providers will be automatically checked by custom applications. Any files that do not meet the core minimum requirements will be returned to the producer to be remedied and re-submitted.

This paper will discuss the header requirements for TIFF images included in the American Memory Web site, which are still in effect (and also used by Global Gateways, a program that came along later). It will also list the TIFF tags required National Digital Newspaper Program (NDNP) as detailed in the NDNP TIFF Profile.

7.6.2. OCR and Retaining Page Layout

Optical Character Recognition (OCR) : The latest versions of both Xerox's TextBridge and Caere's Omnipage incorporate technology allow the option of maintaining text and graphics in their originallay out as well as plain ASCII and word-processing formats. Output can also include HTML with attributes like bold, underline, and italic retained.

Retaining Layout after OCR : Several software packages now offer facility of retaining the page layout after it has been OCR ed. The process for retaining the page layout is software dependent. Caere's Omnipro offers two ways of retaining page layout following OCR. It calls them True Page Classic and True Page Easy. True Page Classic places each paragraph within a separate frame of a word processor into which the OCR output IS saved. If one wishes to edit anything subsequently, then the relevant paragraph box may need to ber6sized. However, 'Easy Edit' facilitates editing of pages without the necessity of resizing the boxes although there is a greater chance of spillage over the page. Xerox TextBridge offers similar feature called DocuRT which is broadly equivalent to True PageEasy Edit. The process of OCR dismantle the page, OCR it, and then reassemble it in such as way that all the component parts such as tabs, columns, table, graphics can be used in a text manipulation package such as word processor.

The process of OCR results in computer-processible file that is less accurate than rekeying-in the data. At an accuracy ratio of 98%, a page having 1800 characters will have 36 error per page on an average. It is therefore, imperative to clean up after OCR unless original scanned image will be viewed as page and OCR being used purely for creating a searchable index on the words that will be searched via a fuzzy retrieval engine like Excalibur which is highly tolerant to OCR errors.

Another possibility for cleaned-up OCR is use of specialist OCR system such as Prime Recognition. With production OCR in mind, Prime OCR licenses leading recognizing engine and passes the data through several of them using voting technology along with artificial intelligent algorithms. The use of multiple OCR engines improves the result achieved by a single engine by 65-80 %. The technology is available at price depending upon number of search engine that one would like to incorporate. Michigan Digital Library production services used Prime OCR for placing more than two million pages of SGML-encoded text and the same number of page images on the web.

7.6.3. Retaining Page Layout Using Acrobat Capture

The Acrobat Capture 2.0 provides several options for retaining not only the page layout but also the fonts, and to fit text into the exact space occupied in the original, so that the scanned and OCRed copy never over- or under-shoots the page. Accordingly, it treats unrecognizable text as pasted-in images, which are perfectly readable by anyone looking at the PDF file, but which will be absent from the editable and searchable text file. In contrast, ordinary OCR programs treat unrecognized text as tildes or some other special character in the ASCII output. Acrobat Capture can be used to scan pages as images, image+text and as normal PDF, all the three options retain page layout.

Image only : Image only option has already been described in option 1.

Image+Text : In image+text solutions, a OCRed text is generated for each image where each page is an exact replica of the original and left untouched, however, the

OCRed text sits behind the image and is used for searching. The OCRed text is generally not corrected for errors since it is used only for searching. The cost involved is much less than PDF Normal. However, the entire page is a bitmap and neither fonts nor line drawings are vectorised, so the file size of Image + Text PDFs is considerably larger than the corresponding PDF Normal files and pages will not display as quickly or cleanly onscreen.

PDF Normal : POF normal gives the clearest on-screen display, is searchable, and yet with significantly smaller file size than Image+Text. The result is not, however, an exact replica of the scanned page. While all graphics and formatting are preserved, substitute fonts maybe used where direct matches are not possible. It is a good choice when files need to be posted to the web or otherwise delivered online. If, during the capture and OCR process, a word cannot be recognized to the specified confidence level, capture, by default, substitutes it with a small portion of the original bitmap image. Capture's 'best guess' of the suspect word lies behind the bitmap so that searching and indexing are still possible. However, one cannot guarantee that these bit-mapped words are correctly guessed. In addition, the bit-map is somewhat obtrusive, detracting from the 'look' of the page. Further, capture provides option to correct suspected errors left as bit-mapped image or leave them untouched.

7.6.4. Re - Keying the Data

A classic solution of this kind would comprise of keying-in the data and its verification. This involves a complete keying of the text, followed by a full rekeying by a different operator, the two keying-in operation might take place simultaneously. The two keyed-in files are compared and any errors or inconsistencies are corrected. This would guarantee at least 99.9% accuracy, but to reach 99.955% accuracy level, it would normally require full proof-reading of the keyed-in files, plus table lookups and dictionary spell checks.

7.7. SUMMARY

With the technology available at an affordable cost, the libraries can initiate small digitization projects as individual library or as a group of libraries. Building-up digital collection and infrastructure required to access them is a challenge that every library has to deal with.

Recent growth and development in digital libraries can broadly be grouped into three broad categories, i.e., (a) digitization of traditional. Printed-resources and their integration with secondary sources of information like Medline. Most of the secondary services now incorporate link to the full text articles on the publisher's site. Developments of platforms lie Cross ref, Web of Science, Silver Linker, etc. are indication of trends towards gradual merger of full text resources and secondary services; (b) digital library derived from the data files generated as a byproduct in the process of printing of primary journals or major reference works. Most of the publishers of STM journals have launched their digital collections consisting of electronic counter-parts of their printed journals; and (c) new information sources that are created especially for the web imbibing frill of technological advances. The numbers and variety of resources in the last category are expected to increase as the users respond to technologically advanced products and services. The meaning of digital library is in the process of evolution as it climbs along the technological ladder.

It can thus be concluded that further advances in the area of digital libraries would rest upon further technological developments as well as conceptual foundation that is being laid down presently.

Unlike microfilming, digital imaging technologies present a preservation solution for the documents in libraries with increased accessibility over the electronic networks, high quality output, OCRed text, electronic links to individual pages, etc. However, imaging technologies are still in a continuous flux of change. New standards and protocols are being defined on a regular basis for file formats, compression techniques, hardware components, network interfaces, etc. The librarian should be aware of constant threat of 'techno-obsolescence' and transitory standards. Magnetic and optical discs as a physical media are re-engineered to store more and more data. There is a constant threat of backward compatibility for the products that were used in the past. Acquiring an imaging system with all its peripherals capable of enhancing access to the library resources is quite a simple task especially now that the cost of all computing systems and peripherals are crashing down. However, the libraries must be concerned with all aspects of imaging technologies, as well as new demands that the technology will place on them as an organisation.

Digital images will have to be constantly migrated converted to new formats computing devices, storage media and software as new forms of storage devices, updated formats and software and improved computing systems are released. In spite of the fact that this constant migration conversion of digital images would not only be expensive it would also direct valuable manpower resources into a constant re-invention of wheel, it would be essential to do so otherwise valuable images data would be left behind an obsolete machinery which will eventually break down rendering data inaccessible.

7.8. REVIEW QUESTIONS

1. Define 'Digitization'.
2. Discuss the need for digitization.
3. What are the factors to be considered before selecting different media for digitization?

8
Methods and Equipment

STRUCTURE

8.0. OBJECTIVES

- To have a look for the current digitization status among the libraries of special concern to the university libraries.
- To examine different constraints of digitization
- To examine the infrastructural facilities required for digital information system (Scanner, computer, software, OCR,).
- To discuss various file formats and media types of digitization

8.1. INTRODUCTION

Digitization is the process of converting the content of physical media (e.g. periodical articles, books, manuscripts, cards, photographs, vinyl disks, etc.) into digital format. In most library applications, digitization normally results in a document that are accessible from the web site of a library, and thus on the Internet. Optical scanners and digital cameras are used to digitise images by translating them into bit maps. It is also possible to digitise sound, video, graphics, animations etc. Digitization is not an end in itself. It is the process that creates a digital image from an analogue image. Selection criteria, particularly those which reflect user needs, are of paramount importance. Therefore, the principles that are applicable in traditional collections development are applicable when materials are being selected for digitization. However, there are several other considerations related to technical, legal, policy, and resources that become important in a digitization project.

Digitization is one of the three important methods of building digitised collections. The other two methods include providing access to electronic resources (whether free or licensed) and creating library portals for important Internet resources. In this unit let us discuss the technology of digitization, tools, methods, scanners, etc.

8.2. TECHNOLOGY OF DIGITIZATION

Digital images, also called "bit-mapped page image" are "electronic photographs" composed or set of bits or pixels (picture elements) represented by "0" and "1". A bit mapped page image is a true representation of its original in terms of typefaces, illustrations, layout and presentation of scanned documents.

As such information contents of "bit-mapped page image" cannot be searched or manipulated unlike text file documents (or ASCII). However, an ASCII file can be generated from a bit-mapped page image using optical character recognition (OCR) software such as Xerox's TextBridge and Care's OmniPage. The quality of digital image can be monitored at the time of capture by the following factors:

- Bit depth / dynamic range
- Resolution
- Threshold
- Image enhancement

Before taking-up the above mentioned technological aspects, let us understand important terminology associated with them.

Bit and Byte : Bit is short for binary digit, the smallest unit of information on a machine. A single bit can hold only one of two values: 0 or 1. More meaningful information is obtained by combining consecutive bits into larger units. A byte is composed of 8 consecutive bits.

Pixels : The term "pix" means "part of a picture" and "el" means "from element". In bitonal (black and white) display, each pixel can have only one bit, i.e. either black or white, whereas in a grey-scale display, each pixel can have three numerical values for three colours, i.e. Red, Green, and Blue (RGB) to represent the colour. These three RGB components can be represented by three 8-bitnumbers for each pixel. Three 8-bit bytes (one byte for each of RGB) is called24 bit colour. Each 8 bit RGB component can have 256 possible values, ranging from 0 to 255. For example, three values like (250, 165, 0), meaning (Red=250, Green=165, Blue=0) to denote one Orange pixel. The pixels are most commonly used to represent images as a computer file. Pixels are of a uniform size and shape.

8.2.1. Bit Depth on Dynamic Range

The number of bits used to define each pixel determines bit depth. The greater the bit depth, the greater the number of grey scale or colour tones that can be represented.

Dynamic range is the term used to express the full range of total variations, as measured by a densitometer between the lightest and darkest of a document. Digital images can be captured at varied density or bits pixel depending upon:

(i) The nature of source material or document to be scanned

(ii) Target audience or users

(iii) Capabilities of the display and print subsystem that are to be used.

Bitonal or black and white or binary scanning is generally employed in libraries to scan pages containing text or the drawings. Bitonal or binary scanning represents one bit per pixel (either "0" (black) or "1" (white). Grey scale scanning is used for reliable reproduction of intermediate or continuous tones found in black and white photographs to represent shades of grey. Multiple numbers of bits ranging from 2-8 are assigned to each pixel to represent shades of grey in this process. Although each bit is either black or white, as in the case of bitonal images, but bits are combined to produce a level of grey in the pixel that is black, white or somewhere in between lastly colour scanning can be employed to scan colour photographs. As in the case of grey-scale scanning, multiple bits per pixels typically 2 (lowest quality) to 8 (highest quality) per primary colour are used for representing colour. Colour images are evidently more complex than grey scale images, because, it involves encoding of shades of each of the three primary colours, i.e., red, green and blue (RGB). If a coloured image is captured at 2 bits per primary colour, each primary colour can have 22 or 4 shades and each pixel can have 43 shades for each of the three primary colour. Evidently, increase in bit depth increases the quality of image captured and the space required to store the resultant image. Generally speaking, 12 bits per pixel (4 bits per primary colour) is considered minimum pixel depth for good quality colour image. Most of today's colour scanner can scan at 24-bit colour (8 bit per primary colour).

8.2.2. Resolution

DPI, which is a paper dots per inch, does count when scanning. When an image is scanned, one scanning "dot" equals one digital image pixel. You are converting an object with physical dimensions to digital pixel dimensions.

Before you do your first scan, you'll want to know what DPI the paper object (a printed photo for example) should be scanned at. There are a couple of ways at looking at this:

1. You can simply pick a number that will provide a good quality scan with a reasonable file size. This is usually about 600 dpi. That will provide enough pixels to effectively double (or triple) the potential output size while maintaining photographic quality.
2. You can calculate the dpi of the scan based on your desired output size. For instance, say you wanted to scan a 4" x 6" inch photo with a desire to later be able to print it at 8.5" x 11". First, choose your desired ppi for the final print - although 200 is likely sufficient, most print shops are going to ask for 300 - so let's choose 300 ppi.

To get an 8.5" x 11" print at 300 ppi, you're going to need a digital image that is 2550 (8.5 x 300) by 3300 (11 x 300) pixels in size. To scan 4 inches to 2550 pixels will require a DPI of 638 (2550 divided by 4). To scan 6 inches to 3300 pixels will require a DPI of 550 (3300 divided by 6).

The two DPIs are not the same since the aspect ratio of the two print sizes is different. The rule is to simply pick the largest DPI number - in this case 638 (you can round up to say 650 since a bit bigger are okay). Your 4" x 6" photo scanned at 650 dpi will result in a digital image that is 2600 x 3900 pixels in size. With cropping, the digital image will print to 8.5" x 11" at 306 ppi.

SVGA includes an array of computer display standards utilized for the manufacturing of computer monitors and screens. It features a screen resolution of 800x600 pixels.

Monitors that use the SVGA graphic standard are intended to perform better than normal VGA monitors.

SVGA monitors make use of a VGA connector (DE-15 a.k.a HD-15).

A VGA monitor generally displays graphics in 640x480 pixels, or may be an even smaller 320x200 pixels while SVGA monitors display a better resolution of 800x600 pixels or more.

When comparing SVGA with other display standards like Extended Graphics Array (XGA) or VGA, the standard resolution of SVGA is identified as 800x600 pixels.

The SVGA standard was referred to as a graphic resolution of 800x600 4-bit pixel (48000 pixels) when it was initially defined. This implies that every single pixel can be one of 16 different colors. Later, this definition was extended to a resolution of 1024x768 8-bit pixel, which means that there is a selection of 256 colors.

8.2.3. Threshold

The threshold setting in bitonal scanning defines the point on a scale, ranging from 0 (black) to 255 (white), at which the gray values captured will be converted to black or white pixels. Note the effect of varying the threshold on typescript scanned at the same resolution on the same scanner.

Sample A *Sample B*

Effects of Threshold on Resolution: Sample A has a lower threshold (60) than Sample B (100).

Threshold:

1. The beginning point of something
2. The point at which a stimulus is just strong enough to produce a response...

For DTP and Prepress personnel, threshold can be the name given to a control in scanning software or in an option window used for converting existing grey scale pixels to black or white 1Bit line image pixels.

It would then be a situation where software would have to decide that if the grey value of a pixel was equal to or more than the threshold value, then that pixel has to be given a new value of 0 (RGB black) and if the pixel grey value was less than the threshold value, that pixel would be given a value of 255 (RGB white). And so it would go on through every pixel in the image.

Even when we scan a line copy and select the 'Scan to Line' or 'Scan to B/W' option, the light sensitive array of CCDs (using a flatbed scanner) will only "see" variations in light strength and send to the internal components, variations in electrical current that will be converted to one of the many grey colour values that the scanner can support (i.e. 256) - for each CCD created pixel. This never varies; a digital scanner always produces grey values.

Then either the scanners inbuilt software or, in the case of a programs conversion option, program algorithms will have to decide at what colour value (the threshold) pixels become either black or white. (User controls might present the range as 0% to 100%, or 8bit 0 to 255)

8.2.4. Image Enhancement

Enhancement processes improve scanning quality but their use raises concerns about fidelity and authenticity. Many institutions argue against enhancing master images, limiting it to access files only. Typical enhancement features in scanner software or image editing tools include descreening, despeckling, deskewing, sharpening, use of custom filters, and bit-depth adjustment. Here are several examples of image enhancement processes.

Image enhancement process can be used to improve scanned images at a cost of image authenticity and fidelity. The process of image enhancement is, however, time consuming, it requires special skills and would invariably increase the cost of conversion. Typical image enhancement features available in a scanning or image editing software include filters, tonal reproduction, curves and colour management, touch, crop, image sharpening, contrast, transparent background, etc. In a page scanned in grey scale, the text /line art, and half tone areas can be decomposed and each area of the page can be filtered separately to maximize its quality. The text area on page can be treated with edge sharpening filters so as to clearly define the character edges, a second filter could be used to remove the high-frequency noise and finally another filter could fill-in broken characters. Grey-scale area of the page could be processed with different filters to maximize the quality of the halftone.

8.3. COMPRESSION

Lossy compression can have a pronounced impact on image quality, especially if the level of compression is high. In general, the richer the file, the more efficient and sustainable the compression. For instance, a bitonal scan of a page at 600 dpi is 4 times larger than a 300 dpi version, but often only twice as large in its compressed state. The more complex the image, the poorer the level of compression that can be obtained in a lossless or visually lossless state. With photographs, lossless compression schemes often provide around a 2:1 file size ratio; with lossy compression above 10 or 20:1, the effect may be obvious.

8.3.1. Lossless Compression

The conversion process converts repeated information as a mathematical algorithm that can be decompressed without losing any details into the original image with absolute fidelity. No information is "lost" or "sacrificed" in the process of compression. Lossless compression is primarily used in bitonal images.

8.3.2. Lossy Compression

The goal of lossless image compression is to represent an image signal with the smallest possible number of bits without loss of any information, thereby speeding up transmission and minimizing storage requirements. The number of bits representing the signal is typically expressed as an average bit rate (average number of bits per sample for still images, and average number of bits per second for video). The goal of lossy compression is to achieve the best possible fidelity given an available communication or storage bit rate capacity or to minimize the number of bits representing the image signal subject to some allowable loss of information. In this way, a much greater reduction in bit rate can be attained as compared to lossless compression, which is necessary for enabling many real-time applications involving the handling and transmission of audiovisual information. The function of compression is often referred to as coding, for short.

Lossless compression is possible because, in general, there is significant redundancy present in image signals. This redundancy is proportional to the amount of correlation among the image data samples. For example, in a natural still image, there is usually a high degree of spatial correlation among neighboring image samples. Also, for video, there is additional temporal correlation among samples in successive video frames.

8.4. OCR (OPTICAL CHARACTER RECOGNITION)

OCR is a technology that enables you to convert different types of documents such as scanned paper documents, PDF files or images captured by a digital camera into editable and searchable data. Images captured by a digital camera differ from scanned documents or image. They often have defects such as distortion at the edges and dimmed light, making it difficult for most OCR applications, to correctly recognize the text. We have chosen Tesseract because of wide spread approbation, its extensibility and flexibility, its community of active developers, and the fact that it "just works" out of the box.

OCR (Optical Character Recognition) programs are software tools used to transform scanned textual page images into word processing file. OCR or text recognition is the process of electronically identifying text in a bit-mapped page image or set of images and generate a file containing that text in ASCII code or in a specified word processing format leaving the image intact in the process. The OCR is performed in order to make every word in a scanned document readable and fully searchable without having to key in everything in the computer manually. Once a bit-mapped page image has gone through the process of OCR, a document can be manipulated and managed by its contents, i.e. using the words available in the text.

OCR does not actually convert an image into text but rather creates a separate file containing the text while leaving the image intact. There are four types of OCR technology that are prevailing in the market. These technologies are: matrix matching, feature extraction, structural analysis and neural networking.

Matrix/Template Matching : Compares each character with a template of the same character. Such a system is usually limited to a specific number of fonts, or must be "taught" to recognise a particular font.

Feature Extraction : Can recognise a character from its structure and shape (angles, points, breaks, etc.) based on a set of rules. The process claims to recognise all fonts.

Structural analysis : Determines characters on the basis of density gradations or character darkness.

Neural Networking : Neural networking is a form of artificial intelligence that attempts to mimic processes of the human mind. Combined with traditional OCR techniques plus pattern recognition, a neural network based system can perform text recognition and "learn" from its success and failure. Referred to as "Intelligent Character Recognition", a neural network-based system are being used to recognize hand-written text as well as other traditionally difficult source material. Neural network ICR can contemplate characters in the context of an entire word. Newer ICR combines neural networking with fuzzy logic.

Text images are processed with OCR software and hardware. The process involves three operations: document analysis (extracting individual character images),recognizing these images based on i) their template stored in the OCR database; ii) structure and shape (angles, points, breaks, etc.) iii) density gradations or character darkness and iv) contextual processing. The output interface is responsible for communication of OCR system results to the outside world.

Several software packages now offer facility of retaining the page layout after it has been OCRed. The process for retaining the page layout is software dependent. Caere's Omnipro offers two ways of retaining page layout following OCR. It calls them True Page Classic and True Page Easy. True Page Classic places each paragraph within a separate frame of a word processor into which the OCR output is saved. If one wishes to edit anything subsequently, then the relevant paragraph box may need to be resized. However, Easy Edit facilitates editing of pages without the necessity of resizing the boxes although there is a greater chances of spillage over the page. Xerox Text Bridge offers similar feature called DocuRT which is broadly equivalent to True Page Easy edit. The process of OCR dismantle the page, OCR it, and then reassemble it in such a way that all the component parts such as tabs, columns, table, graphic scan be used in a text manipulation package such as word processor.

There is a little doubt about the fact that OCR is less accurate than rekeying-in the data. At an accuracy ratio of 98%, a page having 1800 characters will have36 wrong per page on an average. It is therefore, imperative to clean up after OCR unless original scanned image will be viewed as page and OCR is being used purely to create a searchable index on the words that will be searched via a fuzzy retrieval engine like Excalibur which is highly tolerant to OCR errors.

8.5. FILE FORMATS AND MEDIA TYPES

File format is one of the core issues in any digital preservation approach. Digital information is produced in a variety of standard and proprietary formats, including ASCII, common image formats, word processing, spreadsheets, database documents, formulae, charts, multimedia files and sound and video. As a result of such a heterogeneous nature of storable information, a high number of file formats are now spread, and many of them often need specific software to view or edit the file. These formats are continuously evolving and becoming more complex due to new features and functionality. Before preserving digital records it is necessary to know in which file format the digital record is created. For example, to view an older word processing file, one needs software that understands the encoding schemes of the original software and can display that properly on the screen .Thus several factors need to be considered while adding any document in digital repository.

8.5.1. Formats and Encoding Used for Text

Text-based contents of a digital library can be stored and presented as i) simple text or ASCII(American Standard Code for Information Interchange; ii) unstructured text; and iii) Structured text(SGML or HTML or XML); iv) page description language; and v) page image formats.

Simple text or ASCII : Simple text or ASCII (American Standard Code for Information Exchange) is the most commonly used encoding scheme used for facilitating exchange of data from one software to another or from one platform to another. "Full-text" of articles from many journals has been available electronically through online vendors like DIALOG and STN in this format for over two decades. Typically what is stored in the text of each article, broken into paragraphs, along with bibliographic information is a simple tagged information.

Simple text or ASCII is compact, economic to capture and store, searchable, inter-operable and is malleable with other text-based services. On the other hand, the simple text or ASCII cannot be used for displaying complex tables or mathematical formulas, photographs, diagrams, graphics; special characters cannot be displayed in ASCII. ASCII format does not store text formatting information, i.e. italics, bold, font type, font size or paragraph justification information. Simple text or ASCII in many ways is inadequate to represent many journal articles because of the reasons mentioned above. Although simple text or ASCII is extremely useful for searching and selection, its inability to capture the richness of the original makes it an interim step to structured text formats.

Structured text : Structured text attempt to capture the essence of documents by "marking-up" the text so that the original form could be recreated or even produce other forms such as ASCII. Structured text format have provision to imbed images, graphics and other multimedia formats in the text. SGML (Standard Generalized Markup Language) is one of the most important and popular structured text format. ODA (Office Document Architecture) is a similar and competing standard. SGML is an international standard (ISO, 1986) around which several related standards are built. SGML is flexible language that gave birth to HTML (Hyper-text Markup Language), de facto markup language of the World Wide Web, to control the display format of documents and even the appearance of the user interface for interacting with the documents. Extensible Markup Language (XML) is derived from SGML to interchange structured documents on the web. Like SGML, XML also deals with the structure of document and not its formatting. The Cascading Style Sheet (CSS) developed for HTML would also function for XML to take care of formatting and appearance. Unlike HTML, XML allows for the invention of new codes. Unlike SGML, XML always requires explicit end tags that make it a lot easier to write tools and browsers.

Like simple text or ASCII, structured text can be searched or manipulated. It is highly flexible and suitable both for electronic and paper production. Well-formatted text increase visual presentation of textual, graphical and pictorial value of information. Structured formats can easily display complex tables and equations. Moreover, the structured text is compact in comparison to the image-based formats, even after including imbedded graphics and pictures.

Besides SGML and HTML, there are other formats used in digital library implementation. TeX, used for formatting highly mathematical text is one such format which allows greater control over the resulting display of document, including reviewing the formatting of errors.

Page Description Language (PDL) : Page Description Language (PDLs), such as Adobe's PostScript and PDF (Portable Document Format) are similar to image but the formatted pages displayed to the user are text-based rather than image based. PostScript and PDF formats can easily be captured during the typesetting process. PostScript is especially easy to capture since most of the systems automatically generate it and conversion program, called Acrobat Distiller, can be used to convert PostScript file into PDF files. The documents stored as PDF require Acrobat Reader at the user's end to read or print the document. The Acrobat Reader can be downloaded free of cost from the Adobe's Web Site.

Acrobat's Portable Document Format (PDF) is a by-product of PostScript, Adobe's page-description language that has become the standard way to describe pages electronically in the graphics world. While PostScript is a programming language, PDF is a page-description format.

Page Image Format : The digitally scanned images are stored in a file as a bit-mapped page image, irrespective of the fact that a scanned page contains a photograph, a line drawing or text. The bit-mapped page image can be created in dozens of different formats depending upon the scanner and its software. National and international standards for image-file formats and compression methods exist to ensure that data will be interchangeable amongst systems. An image file stores discrete sets of data and information allowing a computing system to display interprets and prints the image in a pre-defined fashion. An image file format consists of three district components, i.e. header which stores information on file identifier and image specifications; Image data consisting of look-up table and image raster and lastly footer that signal file termination information. While bit-mapped portion of a raster image is standardized, it is the file header that differentiates one format from another.

TIFF (Tagged Image File Format) is the most commonly used page image file format and is considered to be the de facto standard for bitonal images. Some image formats are propriety developed by a commercial vendor and require a specific software or hardware for display and printing. Images can be coloured, grey-scale or black and white (called bitonal). They can be uncompressed (raw) or compressed using several different compression algorithms.

Image files are much larger than text files, thus compression is necessary for their economic storage. A compression algorithm reduces a redundant string such as one or more rows of white bits, to a single code. The standard compression scheme for black and white bitonal image is the one developed by the International Telecommunications Union (formerly Consultative Committee for International Telephony & Telegraphy

(CCITT) for group 4 fax images, commonly referred to as CCITT Group 4(G-4) or ITU-G-4. An image created as a TIFF and compressed using CCITT Group 4 is called a TIFF G4 which is the de facto standard for storing bitonal images. Some of the formats mentioned above are maintained and developed by international organizations such as the International Standards Organization (ISO), the International Telecommunications Union (ITU).

8.6. TOOLS OF DIGITIZATION

Digital imaging is an inter-linked system of hardware, software, image database and access sub-system with each having their own components. Tools used for digitization include several core and peripheral systems. An image scanning system may consist of a stand-alone workstation where most or all the work is done on the same workstation or as a part of a network of workstations with imaging work distributed and shared amongst various workstations. The network usually includes a scanning station, a server and one or more editing, retrieval stations. A typical scanning workstation for a small, production level project could consist of the following:

- Hardware (Scanners, computers, data storage and data output peripherals)
- Software (image capturing and image editing)
- Network (data transmission)
- Display and Printing technologies

This Unit concentrates on scanners and scanning software as important components of the scanning system.

8.6.1. Scanners: How does a Scanner Work?

Digital scanners are used to capture digital images from analogue media such as printed pages or a microfiche / microfilm at a predefined resolution and dynamic range (bit range). There are two types of image scanners: vector scanner and raster scanners. The vector scanners scan an image as a complex set of x, y coordinates. Vector images are generally used in Geographical Information Systems (GIS). The display software for the vector image interprets the image as function of coordinates and other included information to produce an electronic replica of the original drawing or photograph. Vector images can be zoomed in portion to display minute details of a drawing or a map. Maps, engineering drawings, and architectural blueprints are often scanned as vector images. Raster images are captured by raster scanners by passing lights (laser in some cases) down the page and digitally encoding it row by row. Multiple passes of lights may be required to capture basic (as a set of bits known as bit map) colours in a coloured image.

Raster scanners are used in libraries to convert printed publications into electronic forms. Majority of electronic imaging systems generate raster images. The scanners used for digitizing analogue images into digital images come in a variety of shapes and sizes.

How Scanner Works?

Scanners are equipped with a lamp that moves with the scanner head to light-up the object being scanned. Most scanners use a cold cathode florescent lamp or a xenon lamp. The scan head is made up of the mirrors, lens, filter, and charge-coupled devices (CCD) array. A belt that is connected to the stepper motor makes the scan head move. A stabilizing bar prevents wobbling during the pass. The mirrors reflect what is being scanned into the lens and the image is then focused through a filter on the CCD array. Three smaller images of the original are made by the lens. These images then go through a color filter and onto a section of the CCD array. The data is then combined into a single image.

While selecting a scanner, one should consider resolution, sharpness, and rate of image transfer. The resolution is measured in dots per inch (dpi). The average scanner has at least 300x300 dpi. The number of sensors in a row of the CCD array determines a scanner‘s dpi. Sharpness depends on how bright the lamp is and the quality of the lens. Image transfer depends on the connection used to connect the scanner to the computer. The slowest is the parallel port. Universal Serial Bus or USB scanners are affordable, easy to use, and have good speed.

The hardware required for a scanner is a connector such as a USB. The software required is a driver. The driver is needed to communicate with the scanner. TWAIN is the language spoken by scanners. Any program that supports TWAIN can acquire a scanned image.

8.7. TYPES OF SCANNERS

There are following types of Scanners:

- Flatbed Scanners – right angle, prism and overhead flatbed
- Sheet-Feed Scanners
- Drum Scanners
- Digital Cameras
- Slide Scanners
- Microfilm Scanners
- Video Frame Grabbers
- Hand-held scanners

The type of scanner selected for an imaging project would be influenced by the type, size and source of documents to be scanned. Many scanners can handle only transparent material, whereas others can handle only reflective materials.

8.7.1. Flatbed Scanners

Flatbed scanners are most common, and widely used scanners that look like a photocopier and are used in much the same way. Source material in a flatbed scanner is placed face down for scanning. The light source and charge-coupled devices (CCDs) move beneath the platen, while the document remains stationary as in the case of photocopying machine. Flatbed scanner comes in various models like right-angle, prism and planetary/overhead to handle bound volumes and books. Flatbed scanner can scan usually a document at 600 dpi. Many flatbed scanners however, offer higher resolution.

8.7.2. Sheet Feed Scanners

In a sheet-feed scanner, as is indicated in the name, document is fed over a stationary CCD and light source via roller, belt, drum, or vacuum transport. In contrast to a flat-bed scanner, sheet-feed scanner has optional attachment of auto- feed uniform-sized stack of documents to be scanned.

8.7.3. Drum Scanners

Source material in a drum scanner is wrapped on a drum, which is then rotated past a high-intensity light source to capture the image. Drum scanners offer superior image quality, but require flexible source material of limited size that can be wrapped around the photosensitive drum. Drum scanners are specially targeted for graphic arts market. Drum scanners offer highest resolution for grey scale and colour scanning. Drum Scanner uses Photo-Multiplier (Vacuum) Tubes (PMTs) instead of CCDs, which offer a greater bit depth (12 to 16 bits).

8.7.4. Digital Cameras

Digital cameras mounted on copy cradle resemble microfilming stand. Source material is placed on the stand and the camera is cranked up or down in order to focus the material within the field of view. Digital cameras are most promising scanner development for library and archival applications.

8.7.5. Slide Scanners

Slide scanners have a slot in the side to accommodate a 35mm slide. Inside the box, the light passes through the slide to hit a CCD array behind the slide. Slide scanners can generally scan only 35mm transparent source materials.

8.7.6. Microfilm Scanner

Specially targeted to library/archival application, microfilm scanners have adapters to convert roll film, fiche, and aperture cards into the same model.

8.7.7. Video Frame Grabber or Video Digitiser

Video digitisers are circuit boards placed inside a computer and attached to a standard video camera. Anything that is filmed by the video camera is digitised by the video digitiser.

8.7.8. Hand-held Scanners

Hand-held scanners are used for scanning selective sections of data. It may require multiple pass to capture large area. Moreover, a user should have a steady hand while moving the scanner over the document to be scanned. These scanners are normally used for circulation work in a library.

8.8. SCANNING SOFTWARE

The scanning software can broadly be categorised into the following three types:

- Scanning Software
- Image Editing Application
- Digitization of audio and video

This software is discussed in the following section.

The scanning software is used for scanning the image and capturing it in the computer. This software is provided by the manufacturer of the product to the buyers. These drivers translate the instructions into commands, which the scanner understands.

8.8.1. Image Editing Applications

Image editing applications are used once the process of scanning the image is over and the image is available in the computer for further manipulation. Most image editing software offer features like image editing, sharpening, filter, cropping, colour adjustments, forms conversion, resizing, etc. Most image editing software can also be used for capturing the images

8.8.2. Digitization of Audio and Video

The songs or speeches that we generally listen from tape recorders or radio are in an analogue form. The analogue sound tracks can be digitized by attaching an audio player to a system through an audio capture card so as to record the sound to the system. The audio files can be saved as wav, mp3, midi, etc. MP3 format is highly compact and the sound quality is better in comparison to other formats. Audio files can be further processed using noise reduction software. Like audio, video capture also requires a video capture card with input from video cassette player (VCP / VCR), TV antenna, cable or movie camera. The digitised files can be saved as mov, avi, mpg file formats.

8.9. ORGANISING DIGITAL IMAGES

A disc full of digital images without any organisation, browse and search options may have no meaning except for one who created it. Scanned images need to be organised in order to be useful. Moreover, images need to be linked to the associated metadata to facilitate their browsing and searching. The following three steps describe the process of organising the digital images:

Organise the scanned image files into disc hierarchy that logically maps the physical organisation of the document. For example, in a project on scanning of journals, create a folder for each journal, which, in turn, may have folder for each volume scanned. Each volume, in turn, may have a subfolder for each issue. The folder for each issue, in turn, may contain scanned articles that appeared in the issue along with a content page, composed in HTML providing links to articles in that issue.

Name the scanned image files in a strictly controlled manner that reflects their logical relationship. For example, each article may be named after the surname of first author followed by a volume number and an issue number. For example, file name"smithrkv5n1.pdf" conveys that the article is by "R.K. Smith" that appeared in volume 5and issue no.1. The file name for each article would, therefore, convey a logical and hierarchical organisation of the journal.

Describe the scanned images file internally using image header and externally using linked descriptive metadata files. The following three types of metadata are associated with the digital objects:

(i) Descriptive Metadata : Include content or bibliographic description consisting of keywords and subject descriptors.

(ii) Administrative or technical Metadata : Incorporates details on original source, date of creation, version of digital object, file format used, compression technology used, object relationship, etc. Administrative data may reside within or outside the digital object and is required for long-term collection management to ensure longevity of digital collection.

(iii) Structural Metadata : Elements within digital objects facilitate navigation, e.g. table of contents, index at issue level or volume level, page turning in an electronic book, etc.

The simplest and least effective method for providing access is through a table of contents and linking each item to its respective object / image. Content pages of issues of journals done in HTML would offer browsing facility. Full-text search to HTML pages or OCRed pages can be achieved by installing one of the free Internet search engines like OingoFree Search (http://www.oingo.com/oingo_free_search/products.html);Swish-E(http://www.berkeley.edu/SWISH-E/);WhatyoUseek (http://intra.whatuseek.com/); Excite (http://excite.com/) and Google (http://www.google.com).

Large scanning projects would, however, require a back-end database storing images or links to the images and metadata (descriptive / administrative). Back-end database used by most document management systems holds the functionality required by most web applications. Important management systems like File Net have now integrated their database with HTML conversion tools. Further, some of the document management systems have also signed up with Adobe to incorporate Acrobat and Acrobat Capture into their web-based document management systems. These databases entertain queries from users through "HTML forms" and generate search results on the fly. Several digital library packages are now available as "open source" or "free-ware" that can be used not only for organizing the digital objects but also for their search and retrieval.

8.10. DIGITAL LIBRARY SOFTWARE

Several digital library software are currently available like, Greenstone Digital Library (GSDL), Dspace, Eprints, Fedora, etc., which are available freely for download on the Internet. There is some commercial Digital Library Software available but none has been used on large scale in comparison to the ones mentioned above. We will provide here a brief account of digital library softwares available in public domain. The description is an outline of the features of the respective software.

Dspace : Dspace (www.dspace.org) has been developed in partnership between Hewlett Packard (HP) and Massachusetts Institute of Technology (MIT). Development is still in progress but as institutional repository software. Dspace is making its mark, with an increasing number of institutions around the globe installing, evaluating, and using the package. The latest stable version is 1.2 available for download at the Dspace web site. Currently, the original developers undertake most of the core development, but a growing technical user base is generating suggestions for future releases as well as looking for producing some add-on modules. In addition the Dspace Federation is guiding the transition of this software to a more community-wide open-source development model.

Dspace captures, stores, indexes, preserves, and, redistributes the intellectual output of a university's research faculty into digital formats. Dspace accepts all forms of digital materials including text, images, video, and audio files. Possible content includes: articles and preprints; technical reports; working papers; conference papers; e- theses; datasets(statistical, geospatial, matlab, etc.); images (visual, scientific, etc.); audio files; video files; learning objects; and reformatted digital library collections. The back end technologies used include: Apache, Tomcat, OpenSSL/mod_ssl; Java1.3, JSP1.2, Servlet 2.3;PostgreSQL7, JDBC (RDBMS); CNRI handle System5 (persisten ids); Lucene 1.2 (index/ search).

Pre-requisites : Dspace depends upon the Java programming language and the PostgreSQL open source database system. It also requires a number of additional Java- based elements to be installed: Tomcat, which is a Java based server; a number of Java code libraries; and the Ant, a Java compiler. It is recommended that Dspace be installed on a Linux or a UNIX machine. It requires an experienced system administrator to do the prerequisite installation.

E-prints : GNU Eprints 2.x are free software which creates online archives (http://software.eprints.org/). The default configuration creates a research paper archive. With its origin in the scholarly communication movement, e-print default configuration is geared to research papers but it can be adapted to other purposes and content. It was developed in the Intelligent Agents, Multimedia Group at the Electronics and Computer Science Department of the University of Southampton.GNU Eprints are freely distributed to the GNU General Public License. The latest version is 2.3 and is available for download at http://software.eprints.org/download.php

Prerequisites

- Any computer capable of running GNU/Linux or similar operating system. The faster, the better, but any Intel Pentium II processor will give good performance.
- A GNU operating system. GNU/Linux (a very advanced and free UNIX- like operating system) works just fine, and is in fact the development platform
- Apache WWW server
- Perl programming language, also a number of additional modules
- mod_perl module for Apache, which significantly increases the performance of Perlscripts
- My SQL Database

Greenstone Digital Library (http://greenstone.org)

Greenstone Digital Library is open-source software available under the terms of the GNU General Public License. It has the ability to serve digital library collections and build new collections. It provides a new way of organising information and publishing it on the Internet or on CD-ROM. The Greenstone Digital Library software is produced by the New Zealand Digital Library Project at the University of Waikato, and distributed in cooperation with UNESCO and the Humanities Library Project. The New Zealand Digital Library Web site (http://nzdl.org) contains numerous example collections; all created with the Greenstone software, which are publicly available for anyone to peruse The Greenstone runs on Windows and Unix platforms. The distribution includes ready-to-use binaries for all versions of Windows and for Linux. It also includes complete source code for the system, which can be compiled using Microsoft C++ or gcc. Greenstone works with associated software that is also freely available: the Apache Web server and PERL.

Ganesha Digital Library

Ganesha Digital Library version 3.1 (GDL) (http://gdl.itb.ac.id/) is another open source software developed under Indonesian Digital Library Network (IndonesiaDLN). GaneshaDigital Library enables institutions or individuals to share their knowledge and also access and utilise available knowledge in the Indonesian 'giant memory' through the network of IndonesiaDLN digital libraries. The software is available in three publisher editions: Personal, Internet Cafe, and Institution. Released under the terms of the GNU GPL,(GNU General Public License).

8.11. SUMMARY

The quality of digital image can be monitored at the time of capture by four factors, namely: i) Bit depth / dynamic range; ii) resolution; iii) threshold; and iv) image enhancement. The unit describes these parameters in detail. Image files are evidently larger than textual files. It is thus necessary to compress image files. Image compression is the process of reducing size of an image by abbreviating the repetitive information such as one or more rows of white bits to a single code. The compression algorithms may be grouped as lossless compression and lossy compression.

Text and image-based contents of a digital library can be stored and presented as: i) simple text or ASCII (American Standard Code for Information Interchange; ii) unstructured text; iii) Structured text (SGML or HTML or XML); iv) page description language; and v) page image formats. This unit describes file formats in digitised collection.

An image scanning system may consist of a stand-alone workstation where most or all the work is done on the same workstation or as a part of a network of workstation with imaging work is distributed and shared amongst various workstations. The network usually includes a scanning station, a server and one or more editing, retrieval stations. A typical scanning workstation for a small, production-level project could consist of the following:

- Hardware (Scanners, computers, data storage and data output peripherals)
- Software (image capturing and image editing)
- Network (data transmission)
- Display and Printing technologies

This unit describes scanners and scanning software as important components of scanning system.

8.12. REVIEW QUESTIONS

1. Explain the four types of OCR technology.
2. What is image compression? Describe the types of image compression.
3. What is scanner? Explain the different type of scanner?
4. What is OCR? Why is it important to OCR a digitised image?

References

- Adubika, T. (2007). Serials Management In Polytechnic Libraries in Nigeria: A Comparative Study of Kaduna Polytechnic And Yaba College of Technology Libraries. Samaru Journal of Information Studies, 7(2), 28-33.
- Arms, W.Y. (1995). Key Concepts in the Architecture of the Digital Library. D-lib Magazine.
- Arms, William Y. (2000). Digital Libraries. The MIT Press: Cambridge, MA.
- Atherton, P. (1980). Handbook for Information Systems and Services. Paris: UNESCO.

- Atherton, P. (1980). Handbook for Information Systems and Services. Paris: UNESCO.

- Available online at
- Badaru, Ayotunde (2012). Serial Publications: A brief overview. Available online athttp://badaru-ayotunde.blogspot.in/2012/10/serial-publications-briefoverview_9220.html
- Breeding, M. (2001). Providing Virtual Reference Service. Information Today. 18(4); 42-43.

- Breeding, M. (2001). Providing Virtual Reference Service. Information Today. 18(4); 42-43.

- Brown, C.D. and Smith,L.S. (1980). Serials: past, present and future. 2nd ed.Birmingham, AL: EBSCO
- Cabeceiras, James (1982). The Multimedia Library. 2nd ed. New York: Academic Press.

- Cabeceiras, James (1982). The Multimedia Library. 2nd ed. New York: Academic Press.

- Chatterjee, A. (1983). Elements of Documentation. Calcutta: Mukherjee Book House. 35.
- Chatterjee, A. (1983). Elements of Documentation. Calcutta: Mukherjee Book House. 35.
- Chowdhury, G. G. (2001). Digital Libraries and Reference Services: Present and Future. Journal of Documentation. 58(3); 258-283.
- Chowdhury, G. G. (2001). Digital Libraries and Reference Services: Present and Future. Journal of Documentation. 58(3); 258-283.
- Chowdhury, G. G. and Chowdhury, S. (2003). Introduction to Digital Library. London: Facet Publishing. 227-240.
- Chowdhury, G. G. and Chowdhury, S. (2003). Introduction to Digital Library. London: Facet Publishing. 227-240.
- Cortez, E.M. and Smorch, T. (1993). Planning Second Generation Automated Library. Westport: Greenwood Press.
- Farrington, Jean Walter (1997). Serials Management in Academic Libraries: A Guide to Issues and Practices. Westpost, London: Greenwood Press.
- Fisher, S. and Rowley, J. (1994). Management Information and Library Management Systems: An Overview. The Electronic Library. 12(2); 149-117.
- Fothergill, Richard and Butchart, Ian (1990). Non - Book Materials in Libraries:A Practical Guide. 3rd ed. London: Clive Bingley.
- Fothergill, Richard and Butchart, Ian (1990). Non - Book Materials in Libraries: A Practical Guide. 3rd ed. London: Clive Bingley.
- Fothergill, Richard and Butchart, Ian (1990). Non - Book Materials in Libraries: A Practical Guide. 3rd ed. London: Clive Bingley.
- Guha, B. (1983). Documentation and Information: Services Techniques and Systems, 2nd ed. Calcutta: World Press. 36-37.
- Guidelines for Serial Treatment at NLM (2000). Available onhttp://www.nlm.nih.gov/tsd/cataloging/sercat.html) (Last visited on 06.06.2014)
- Haigh, S. (1996). Optical Character Recognition (OCR) as a Digitization Technology. Network Notes. no. 37.

- Harrod, L.M. (1987) Harrods Librarian glossary of terms used in Librarianship documentation and the book crafts and reference. Books 6th ed. Aldershot Hans:Gower.
- Haseltine, R. (1994). New Perspectives on Library Management System. Program. 28(2); 53-61.
- Haseltine, R. "New Perspectives on Library Management System". Program. 28.2(1994): 53-61. Print.
- *http://lisp5.epgpbooks.inflibnet.ac.in/chapter/library-automation-cataloguing/Cabeceiras,* James (1982). The Multimedia Library. 2nd ed. New York: Academic Press.
- http://www.ala.org/ (accessed on 09.12.03)
- *http://www.ala.org/alcts/sites/ala.org.alcts/files/content/resources/collect/serials/acqglossary/05seracq_glo.pdf*
- http://www.biblio-tech.com (accessed on 22.12.03)
- http://www.dvddemystified.com/dvdfaq.html (accessed on 09.11.2003).
- http://www.dvddemystified.com/dvdfaq.html (accessed on 09.11.2003).
- http://www.dvddemystified.com/dvdfaq.html (accessed on 09.11.2003).
- http://www.ilsr.com/ (accessed on 22.11.03)
- http://www.infolibrarian.com (accessed on 02.03.04)
- http://www.koha.org (accessed on 12.02.04)
- http://www.libraryhq.com/ (accessed on 02.03.04)
- http://www.librarytechnology.org (accessed on 03.03.04)
- http://www.oss4lib.org (accessed on 12.04.04)
- http://www.state.sc.us/scdah/SEVEN.PDF (accessed on 09.11.2003).
- http://www.state.sc.us/scdah/SEVEN.PDF (accessed on 09.11.2003).
- IFLA. (2004). IFLA Digital Reference Guidelines. Available at: *www.ifla.org* (Accessed on 06.05.04).
- IGNOU – MLIS – E1 (1997). Preservation and Conservation of Library Materials. New Delhi.
- IGNOU – MLIS – E1 (1997). Preservation and Conservation of Library Materials. New Delhi.
- IGNOU – MLIS – E1 (1997). Preservation and Conservation of Library Materials. New Delhi.

- IMLS: A Framework of Guidance for Building Good Digital Collections. (http://www.imls.gov/pubs/forumframework.htm)
- International Standard Serial Number: International identifier for Serials and other continuing resources in the electronic and print world. Available onhttp://www.issn.org/understanding-the-issn/what-is-an-issn/(Last visited on 06.06.2014)
- Jantz, Ronald. (2001). Technological Discontinuities in the Library: Digital Projects That Illustrate New Opportunities for the Librarian and the Library. IFLA Journal 27, 74-77.
- Kenney, Anne R. and Stephen Chapman. (1996). Digital Imaging for Libraries and Archives. Ithaca: Dept. of Preservation and Conservation, Cornell University Library.
- Kent, Allen (ed.) (1975). Encyclopaedia of Library and Information Science. V. 14. 338-445.
- Kessler, Jack. (1996). Internet Digital Libraries: The International Dimension. Boston: Artech House Publishers.
- Lesk, Michael. (1997). Practical Digital Libraries: Books, Bytes and Bucks. San Fransisco: Morgan Kaufmann Publishers.
- Levitan, K. B. (1982). Information Resources as 'Goods' in the Life Cycle of Information Production. JASIS. 33(1), 44-54.
- Librarians' Index to Internet Resources. Available at: www.lii.org (Accessed on 20.03.04).
- MARC Standards: Library of Congress http://www.loc.gov/marc/ (Last visited on06.06.2014)
- McKierman, G. (2001). LiveRef: Available at: *www.public.iastate.edu/~cyberstacks/* (Accessed on 01/03/04).
- Mcqueen J. and Boss, R.W. (1984). Serials Control in Libraries: Automated Options, Library Technology Reports. 89-282.
- Mishra, R.K. (1999). Library Software Selection: An Analysis. IASLIC Bulletin. 44(3); 125-132.
- Mishra, R.K. "Library Software Selection: An Analysis". IASLIC Bulletin. 44.3(1999): 125-132. Print.
- Moulton, P. D. and Stanley, Timothy S. (1989). Hard Disk Quick Reference. Indiana: Que Corporation.

- Moulton, P. D. and Stanley, Timothy S. (1989). Hard Disk Quick Reference. Indiana: Que Corporation
- Moulton, P. D. and Stanley, Timothy S. (1989).Hard Disk Quick Reference. Indiana: Que Corporation.
- Mukhopadhyay, P.S. (2001). The Progress of Library Management Software: An Indian Scenario. Journal of Library Science. 6; 51-69.
- Mukhopadhyay, P.S. "The Progress of Library Management Software: An Indian Scenario". Journal of Library Science. 6 (2001): 51-69. Print.
- Murray, I.R. (1997). Assessing the Effect of New Generation Library Management Systems. Program. 31(4); 313-327.
- Murray, I.R. "Assessing the Effect of New Generation Library Management Systems". Program. 31.4(1997): 313-327. Print.
- Nisonger, T.E. (1988) Management of serials in Libraries. Engle wood: Libraries unlimited, inc. P.1, 307,308,309,310
- Noerr, Peter (2000). Digital Library Tool Kit. U.S.A.: Sun Microsystems. (http://www.sun.com/products-n-solutions/edu/libraries/digitaltoolkit.html)
- NorthEast Document Conservation Center. NEDCC Handbook for Digital Projects: A Management Tool for Preservation and Access.
- Oppenheim, Charles (ed) (1988). CD – ROM: Fundamentals and Applications. London: Butterworths.
- Oppenheim, Charles (ed) (1988). CD – ROM: Fundamentals and Applications. London: Butterworths.
- Oppenheim, Charles (ed) (1988). CD – ROM: Fundamentals and Applications. London: Butterworths.
- Ostrow, Stephen. Digitizing Historical Pictorial Collections for the Internet. CLIR Feburary 1998. (http://www.clir.org/pubs/reports/ostrow/pub71.html)
- Purcell, Lee (1995). Super CD – ROM Madness. Indianapolis: Sams Publishing. Rajaraman, V. (2001).Fundamentals of Computers. New Delhi: Prentice Hall of India.
- Purcell, Lee (1995). Super CD – ROM Madness. Indianapolis: Sams Publishing.
- Purcell, Lee (1995). Super CD – ROM Madness. Indianapolis: Sams Publishing.
- Rajaraman, V. (2001). Fundamentals of Computers. New

Delhi: Prentice Hall of India.

- Rajaraman, V. (2001). Fundamentals of Computers. New Delhi: Prentice Hall of India.
- Ranganathan, S.R. (1961). Reference Service. Bombay: Asia Publishing House. Tedd, L. A. (1987). Introduction to Computer Based Library Systems. London: Heyde.
- Rosenfeld, Louis and Morville, Peter (1998). Information Architecture. Cambridge: O'Reilly,
- Rowley, J. (1998). The Electronic Library. London: Library Association Publishing. 313-320.
- Rowley, J. (1998). The Electronic Library. London: Library Association Publishing. 313-320.
- Rowley, J. The Electronic Library. London: Library Association Publishing, 1998. Print.
- Serials Acquisitions Glossary (2005), 3rd edition, revised by Serials Section, Acquisitions Committee Association for Library Collections & Technical Services,
- Simmons, P. and Hopkinson, A. (ed.) (1992). CCF/B: The Common Communication Format for Bibliographic Information. Paris: UNESCO.
- Townsend, Sean, [et. al.]. Digitising History. (*http://hds.essex.ac.uk/g2gp/* digitising_history/index.html)
- Tyson, Jeff. (2003). How Scanners Work: How Stuff Works. (http:// www.howstuffworks.com)
- U.S. National Commission on Libraries and Information Science Home Page. Web. 22 April 2004. < http:// www.nclis.gov.>.
- U.S. National Commission on Libraries and Information Science Home Page. Available at: http://www.nclis.gov. (accessed on 22.02.04).
- Weihs, Jean (et al) (1979). Non - Book Materials: The Organisation of Integrated Collections. Canada: Canadian Library Association.
- Weihs, Jean (et al) (1979). Non - Book Materials: The Organisation of Integrated Collections. Canada: Canadian Library Association.
- Weihs, Jean (et al) (1979). Non - Book Materials: The Organisation of Integrated Collections. Canada: Canadian Library Association.

- Whitlatch, J.B. (ed). Reference Futures: Outsourcing, the Web or Knowledge counseling Available at: *www.ala.org/rusa/rusapubs/rusq/contests/contents.htm* (Accessed on 05/04/04).
- William, Saffody. (1989). Introduction to Automation for Librarians. 2nd ed. Chicago: American Library Association. 327-50.
- Yates, R. (1996). Library Automation: The Way Forward? Program. 30(3); 239-53.
- Yates, R. "Library Automation: The Way Forward"? Program. 30.3(1996): 239-53. Print http://www.state.sc.us/scdah/SEVEN.PDF (accessed on 09.11.2003).